SMALL
TALK

SMALL TALK

One Youth. Seven Stories.
Countless Lessons.

JEROME SMALLS

NEW DEGREE PRESS

SMALL TALK:
One Youth. Seven Stories. Countless Lessons.

ISBN   978-1-64137-072-1   *Paperback*
ISBN   978-1-64137-073-8   *Ebook*

PAY IT FORWARD

——

I dedicate this book to every youth in the world without a mentor. To every youth who feels unheard. And to every youth who could use this advice. That's why I'm giving 100% of the proceeds from this book to the My Brother's Keeper Alliance in full support of the work they do.

"Let 'em know you was just like them, but you still rose from that dark place of violence, becoming a positive person. But when you do make it, give back with your words of encouragement. That's the best way to give back."

—Kendrick's Mother

CONTENTS

—

INTRODUCTION

SMALL TALK

———

I first began this overwhelming endeavor of writing my own book as a junior in college only twenty years old—with aspirations of someday having a beard that would finally connect. There were many times when I thought about quitting and giving up on it all. And when I reached the point of no return, there were many times when anxiety would set in and my nerves would consume me. My worry would reach its peak when deadlines from my publisher would approach and I had little to offer, or when I thought my writing began to sound like nonsense. I would ask myself questions like, *What the hell do you think you're doing, bub?* and, *Do you really believe anyone is going to want to read what you have to say?*

I realized I was just a kid—a youth—yet matured and seasoned, tried and true, but a youth nonetheless. Have I lived long enough to share wisdom? Time and time again these thoughts of imposter syndrome would slip into my mind and shake my confidence. And time and time again I would have to remind myself why I began this project in the first place and my courage was restored.

I remember when I first arrived on my college campus and was exposed to a new world of people, a new world of opportunities, but most of all, a new world of truths. It took me nearly twenty full years for it all to start making sense, before I came to understand why I was able to be successful in some areas when sometimes things just weren't meant to be in other areas. It took me twenty years to see how oblivious and flat out lucky I was; yet at the same time, I saw how self-reliant and savvy my younger self was too.

I got to Georgetown University and learned, for the very first time, what it truly meant to be a man of color. I learned what privilege was and how much of it I had acquired, yet how much more I still lacked. I learned what true diversity and inclusion looked like. I learned the amazing influence of music. I learned what it meant to live by conviction and possess passion. I learned the power of self-love. I learned how to forgive those who hurt me the most. And I learned how to pimp my situations, and ultimately, pimp the system (we'll talk more about all of these later).

Needless to say, I discovered a lot about myself when I got to Georgetown, but what angered me the most was that it took me nearly twenty years to be exposed to any of this. Granted, it's safe to say that I grew a great deal during my first year in college, but just like the fourteen-year-old who wakes up four inches taller than when he went to sleep, sometimes it can take months, even years before we get used to our rapid growth.

For natural, healthy growth to be sustainable, it must be done at a regular pace because the truth can be both a soothing sea gently crashing into the banks of our serenity and a raging tsunami on the verge of flooding everything we know. As I came to know more, I placed many pressures and obligations on my shoulders. My growth began to feel more like a tsunami, and in college I almost drowned. How could I have thought I knew so much before coming here, but really knew nothing at all? The better question— the question that infuriated me the most—was why didn't anyone tell me about *any* of these realities before this point?

That's why I wrote this book. My goal is simple: to share the knowledge that took me twenty years to acquire with you, my peers still facing the struggles of college and younger students whose shoes I was just in. Not to be mistaken, I'm not saying I was some ignorant buffoon who knew nothing about anything before coming to college. I don't think I would have made it this far if that were the case. What I am saying is that I never had anyone, in particular, helping me connect life's bigger dots. I never had anyone I could fully relate to, challenging me to question the deeper problems I was facing as a youth.

Ultimately, that's what this book is here to do. It may not change your life forever and open your eyes to everything you never knew—as that would place an extreme amount of pressure on me—but I do believe it will provide you with a fresh perspective and tangible advice from a person who's not too much different from you. I understand what it's like to be depressed and anxious and feel like you don't have anyone to talk to—especially your parents. I get how you can feel unsure about who you are and allow your friends to persuade you to do things you normally wouldn't. And we're not too different in how our energy and our youth drive us to pursue our passions and fight for what we believe in. I get it.

If you're anything like me, you're probably scrappy and possess a level of savviness that has gotten you this far. Before it all became so apparent, I had to figure out most things on my own. In fact, I attribute most of my communication skills and my ability to read any situation, ironically, to me not being able to read in third grade. In elementary school I was so good at math and science that my teachers tended to overlook my illiteracy and pass me along with the mentality of, "oh, he's smart. He'll catch up." Truth be told I'm still catching up. Not knowing how to read is not only embarrassing, but it's also extremely discouraging. That's why I found confidence in learning how to give speeches and having insightful conversations. I became the student who won the vocabulary bee instead of the spelling bee because I realized I didn't need to know how to read a word to know what it means. This also left me with a unique skill set of being able to pick apart and understand nearly every situation I find myself in.

When I didn't know half the words on a page, I became very talented at filling in the gaps, understanding the context, and staying two steps ahead of everyone else so that they never learned I actually started three steps behind. I remember being in Ms. Patterson's world history class in sixth grade, and she would always make us read out loud. I never actually learned anything during these popcorn readings because I'd constantly be counting the people ahead of me to figure out which paragraph would be mine to read next. I mean, how else was I going to not make a fool out of myself when it came to my turn to read out loud? This situation is just one of many ways I've managed to adapt in life.

Kendrick Lamar once asked in an interview, "Do I pimp this situation, or do I fall victim to it?" In a world full of obstacles, oppression, and self-interest, I realized I could only "fall victim" so many times before I began to go insane. So, much like K-Dot, I chose to pimp this situation and others like it.

I share this story because I think it epitomizes how hard I've had to work just to come to know the world around me. Normally, we *learn* so that we can understand. Often times, I had to *understand* before I could learn. In other words, I've always been the kid who needed to know the bigger picture, the "why," before I could understand the smaller pieces of the puzzle. I couldn't fill in the gaps if I didn't know the outline. I'm confident this comes from my illiteracy as a kid and being forced to learn in different ways.

This is a backward process that I don't believe any young person should have to experience. Luckily for me, not all of my learning experiences were always this difficult. As a young, savvy kid I was given many opportunities to let my creativity run wild and my passions fly free. These creative expressions came in the form of recording music with my friends, opting in on final projects instead of final papers, or starting my own business. Through mentorship and the work of nonprofits—one in particular, Youth Entrepreneurship South Carolina (YESCarolina)—I was able to directly benefit from those who invested in youth. My nana, Mrs. Reynolds, Mrs. Zerbst, Jimmy Bailey, Coach Stutts, and countless others saw something in me and that I didn't always see in myself. And even though most of us have individuals like these in our lives, we all internalize these types of personal investments differently.

For me, these investments, leaps of faith, intimate contributions, or whatever you'd like to call them have left me with a passion to give back to the youth in my community. And this term of "my community" means a variety of different things to me. Whether it's the community I identify with, the physical community I reside in, or the Lowcountry community I call home, they all have made an impact on who I am today. Regardless, I established, as a high schooler, that helping my peers and younger students succeed would become my purpose because had it not been for those who helped me, I would have never made it this far.

I've executed this sense of purpose of mine in a lot of different ways. In high school, I got my big break at this when I was given the opportunity to deliver motivational speeches to elementary, middle and high school students. At sixteen-years-old, I found my "why" in life. And it has become both a blessing and curse that drives me every day.

It is a blessing because I know how and where I want to direct my energy, time, and emotions, yet it is also a curse because I know if I'm not able to satisfy this "why," I'll be discontent with everything else I do. In college I've followed my passion by creating my own mentorship organization to empower young men of color in DC, mentoring younger students on campus, teaching fifth graders how to be entrepreneurs, tutoring court-involved youth from the inner-city, shadowing teachers in Southeast DC, and spreading as much knowledge and love as I can to every young person I come across. We all deserve to know and to feel loved, or at least have enough knowledge to even ask the right questions.

That's the purpose of Jerome Smalls, and that's the purpose of this book. I want you to use my stories, my highs as well as my lows, as a frame of reference. I want you to see my vulnerability as an invitation for you to be more vulnerable too because that's what makes us human. I want you to make comparisons between my mistakes and yours and reflect on them to discover new ways of growing. If you are giving something your all (in whatever way you choose), mistakes aren't you *failing*, but you *fostering* a newer version of yourself. I want you to see my words as pieces of a nonconforming puzzle that can be rebranded, reorganized, and reconstructed to fit your specific needs for whatever position you are in your life. I want you to view my advice, not as a map of concrete direction, but as a compass that may guide you throughout your own, unchartered journey. I want what I have to say to challenge you to think differently about your friendships, about your education, about your struggles, and ultimately, about yourself. I want you to see this entire book as a conversation between you and me.

Much like any other conversation, this book doesn't have to be digested all at once. In fact, I don't want you to digest it all in one sitting, and I've structured it accordingly. Each chapter is meant to stand alone as its own nugget of wisdom and advice for you to consume, reflect, and hopefully implement. Every topic is split into three parts: my true story, the context of the issue, and key takeaways.

If you're like my former self, you're not the type of student who necessarily enjoys reading books for leisure. I've written this with you in mind. Not only is it not essential that you read every chapter concurrently, you also have the option to only read what matters to you right now. However, if you are the student who enjoys reading a work cover to cover, this book also keeps you in mind. As you go from one chapter to another and one conversation to the next, you'll be able to pick up the pattern and begin to connect the dots I have scattered across these pages. You will be able to learn more about me while, hopefully, learning about yourself. I wrote this with my heart on my sleeve in hopes that you will feel my authentic voice as you read along.

You'll see, in the very first chapter, my quest for truth and then being motivated to speak that truth. I will explain to you how Kendrick Lamar's music has influenced my way of thinking, how I manipulate my circumstances to work in my favor, and how you can do the same. I'll give you a front row seat to my struggles with love and depression and then show you how I overcame those struggles with positivity and optimism.

You will be able to relate to my tales of mischief and poor judgment as I tell you how the art of peer pressure influenced me. I hope you find inspiration to take more leaps of faith as you claim ownership over your own life. I'll push you to challenge yourself and to not take "no" for an answer, but I'll also caution you to not say "yes" to every request. This book is about you finding your own balance and pace as you embark on your own journey.

I hope you can take away a lot of lessons from this book, but if you learn anything, it should be that this book was not written for me and my agenda. It was written for you.

CHAPTER 1

THE KENDRICK EFFECT

—

TRUE STORY #1

It was the Monday before October 10, 2015. I was nothing but a first-year male student in college, and somehow my naivety had already been taken advantage of. I was the Freshman Representative for the Black Student Alliance (BSA) on campus, and apparently being on the BSA Visions of Excellence Ball planning committee was mandatory. The disorganized weekly meeting ran past its normal 10:00 p.m. end time and I was a little frustrated. I had an essay to write.

My frustration didn't last long, though. This was college. You were supposed to go to meetings, stay up late, and gather with communities you identified with. That's why I joined the BSA. I knew this was an easy way to get accustomed to the "Black community" within such a predominately White institution or PWI. But being Black in college was different than being Black back home in Charleston, South Carolina. Back home, everyone was a part of the Gullah/Geechee culture; so being "Black" only had one definition. It was like we all had one shared experience.

Meanwhile, at college, I was exposed to a different Black diaspora. It was my first time meeting so many African, Afro-Caribbean, and Afro-Latino people. It's hard to explain, but it's almost as if I was more aware of African-American, Southern roots when I got to Georgetown University. What's even worse, it felt like I had to prove my Blackness to the others before I could convince them I deserved to be accepted into their tight-knit community. It was like I had to apply to be a member.

I managed to make it past my first-round interview, but it still surprised me how, with so few Black students here, we were actually quite divided in many regards. Folks seemed to silo themselves based on which part of the diaspora they most identified with. Nevertheless, I played my role well. I mean, there I was, in attendance at that stupid meeting, but it was time for me to leave.

I was halfway out the room when I overheard a conversation between two of the committee members.

"Y'all excited for Georgetown's Homecoming this weekend?" a girl, probably a freshman, asked a group of people still lingering around after the meeting. As a Black college student in DC, at least at Georgetown, it's customary to make sure you specify which homecoming you're talking about, even if it's your school's because we were only four miles away from the mecca of African American higher learning—Howard University. And their homecoming was *The* Homecoming.

"Homecoming? Girl, I ain't going to that. We're probably going to lose anyway. Don't you know the Million Man March is this Saturday?" Alex seemed pretty proud of his weekend plans. He wasn't lying either. Georgetown's football team was weak that year—just like every other year—so they were probably going to lose.

"Oh snap! That's this weekend? I wasn't hip," was the girl's response in an attempt to save face.

"Yeah. A lot of us are going out to the Mall to walk. DC is supposed to be crazy this weekend. Jerome, you going, right?"

He caught me completely off guard. I was just trying to get to the dining hall before Late Night Leo's closed at eleven. I wasn't even a part of their conversation. I couldn't just blow him off, though. I was still submitting my application to the Black community. I actually had planned on going to our Homecoming after my morning shift that Saturday, but this march sounded interesting. I looked at him with a slightly confused face for a brief moment before I answered his question with a question.

"Uhhhhh, what's the Million Man March?"

"What's the Million Ma—" he cut himself off, "Nigga, are you Black?"

Welp, there went my application.

"Don't do him like that!" a different girl, an upperclassman this time, said in my defense. "Not everybody knows about that damn march. They're just freshmen."

Even though her help was condescending, that was my cue to leave before I lodged my foot any further in my mouth. I felt so stupid. What was the Million Man March? At first, I thought it was the protest that Martin Luther King Jr. led in the sixties. That was the only march in DC I had ever heard Black people caring about.

Thank God for Google.

In my search, I realized that I *had* heard of the Million Man March before but I never knew exactly what it was. I was always under the impression this march and MLK's March on Washington were the same thing. I felt almost certain it was taught as if it were the same thing in school (which I couldn't prove, but couldn't disprove either). I knew Black history was always devalued within America's Westernized educational system, but damn, this was frustrating. I was furious. I wasn't even mad at the fact that I didn't know. I was angered by the fact that it felt as though it was purposefully not taught to me.

For those of you who are just as unaware, the Million Man March was a monumental event in Black history. This march is arguably one of the largest gatherings of African Americans to ever take place in this nation (estimates range from 655,000 to over 1.5 million people). I discovered that it was organized by The Nation of Islam minister, Louis Farrakhan, in October of 1995. And that particular Saturday, October 10, 2015, was the march's twentieth anniversary. Black people from across America were coming to take part in it. Farrakhan had called on African Americans from all backgrounds to join together at the National Mall in a peaceful protest for justice and solidarity amongst Black men, just as he did twenty years before.

However, like most historic events, there's always an untold story. This march, both in 1995 and 2015, was said to have brought about much controversy due to Farrakhan's offensive and controversial views. But that's still not enough to justify me not learning about it beforehand.

I remember thinking, *Thomas Jefferson was controversial. Manifest destiny is beyond problematic. And the residual effects of the Reconstruction Era still has an impact on American politics, yet that never stopped any of these topics from being in my textbooks.*

I get it. South Carolina is ranked forty-fifth in the nation for their K-12 public education for a reason, but as I did my research on the Million Man March, there were so many other key events, statistics, and prominent figures within African American culture that I had no clue about. The Million Man March could have been an oversight, but there was no way I was smart enough to get into Georgetown and be so ignorant about my own culture by coincidence. I felt bamboozled. In that moment, I realized I didn't know much about Black history besides Barack Obama, The Civil Rights Movement, George Washington Carver,

Brown v. Board of Education, the 13th Amendment and Harriet Tubman.

To be fair, I couldn't blame my lack of Black knowledge completely on my South Carolina public education. A lot of it had to do with my family upbringing. I was raised by my Black grandfather and White grandmother. My Papa spent most of his time with me teaching me how to work on cars, taking me out fishing, taking me to construction sites, and helping me with my outrageous school projects. He didn't have radical stories of him doing student-ins or joining the Black Panthers movement.

The most he ever had to say was, "Those were different times, and White folks were crazy then," but that was about it.

The only stories I heard from my grandparents regarding anything to do with race was how my great-granddad (Nana's father) was racist and disapproved of their relationship. When I was fourteen years old, Papa and Nana separated, which left Nana to raise me, during some of my most formative years, on her own. Even though she had been with Papa for nearly thirty-five years, she had no real clue about Black history, or why it would be important for me to learn it. And if Papa did have any wisdom to share, he was long gone before I could absorb it.

That Monday night I came to the realization that I didn't know anything (of substance) about my own ancestors' history. Maybe that's why I always felt in limbo when it came to who I was. On one hand, I saw myself as the only one amidst my friends who had a decent "White person voice," wearing sweater vests and being one of two Black kids in my AP classes. On the other hand, I felt most at home at a soulful cookout, watching *The Fresh Prince of Bel-Air*, and making raps with my homies. Either way, I knew I wasn't some privileged kid from the suburbs who was removed from my culture. I'm from the streets and didn't need any pretentious group of people's stamp of approval. I needed my own.

I was inspired to explore further. I figured I had about nineteen years of catching up to do. I read more. I began watching the news with a heightened sense of awareness. Every time a prominent Black figure was mentioned around me that I didn't know, I jotted the name down in my iNotes and Googled him or her later. But school soon got in the way of this. Filling myself in on decades of history was difficult to do while taking seventeen credits. So, I declared myself as an African American Studies minor. I was going to let Georgetown teach me.

I didn't stop there either. I discovered that the easiest way to learn about the culture was to submerge myself in it: the art, the films, and the music, especially the music. I began listening to Erykah Badu, The Stylistics, Miles Davis, Bill Withers, OutKast, Charlie Parker, Donny Hathaway, Earth Wind & Fire, and others. My revised playlist was supplemented by my new college friends. I also expanded my taste in music for current artists to go way beyond the sounds of Rich Homie Quan and Migos. I started listening to musicians like Mick Jenkins, Isaiah Rashad, Bas, Alabama Shakes, Terrace Martin, and Kendrick Lamar. You can probably guess which of them became my favorite.

I appreciated them all, but I fell in love with Kendrick's music. He released his album *To Pimp a Butterfly* five months before the start of my freshmen year. I loved it. I had listened to it plenty of times before I went on this spiritual journey, and his message undeniably meant something to me then, but it didn't *speak* to me until I began seeking the truth. Kendrick had put into words everything I was feeling, literally everything.

He would say things like, "Retraced my steps on what they never taught me. Did my homework fast before government caught me." Or, "I know what I know and I know it well not to ever forget. Until I realized I didn't know shit. The day I came home."

One of K-Dot's lines that stuck with me the most, was in his song "Momma" when he said, "You do know my language. You just forgot because of what public schools have painted. But nevermind, you're here right now, don't you mistake it. It's just a new trip. Take a glimpse of your family ancestor. Make a new list, of everything you thought was progress and that was bullshit."

It's like he took the words right out of my mouth. Would that not trip you out too? Every verse and every metaphor, gave me chills. This was the first time music had ever spoken to me. Granted there were songs that meant something to me and that impacted my life before I discovered Kendrick. But this was the first time music made me question who I was and what I believed in. This was also the first time I applied the lessons from a song to my life. Every time I saw a homeless person, I thought of "How Much Does a Dollar Cost." Every time a cop killed another innocent brown soul, I thought about "The Blacker the Berry." Every time one of my friends conformed to one of the many stereotypes I knew they weren't, I thought about "Institutionalized."

I felt like every time I pressed play I was starting a conversation with him. As if he were talking directly to me. The more I learned, the more I understood his references, and the more I grew, the more I understood the pain he was speaking from. It was like he was trying to help me all along. That's what good rappers do; they take their words and somehow are able to articulate a listener's thoughts, such as mine. That's how they get you. That's how Kendrick got me. *To Pimp a Butterfly* quickly became the soundtrack of my quest for knowledge. It transformed from being music to be being a resource. I'll go as far to say that Kendrick's album changed my life. I think that was because it made me realize how much of life I had left to uncover.

I must sound like a true Kendrick Lamar fanatic right about now, and maybe I am, but I believe I'm destined to be a man of great influence, and every great leader looked up to someone. Martin Luther King admired W.E.B. DuBois and Gandhi. Malcolm X followed the teachings of Marcus Garvey. Plato learned under Socrates. As for me, I'm inspired by Kendrick's message. I feel like his pupil.

Kendrick's vulnerability when expressing his truth has motivated me to do the same. I've probably given upward of one hundred speeches that have reached the ears of thousands since I was in fifth grade, but it wasn't until I got to college and stumbled upon Kendrick Lamar's music, that I began to feel like my authentic self on stage. Before, I used to speak about what I thought people wanted to hear. My most famous lines were:

"Don't let life's speed humps stop you."

"Dare to be different!"

"N.O.W.! — No Opportunities Wasted"

"Only you can fulfill your own shoes."

Don't get me wrong. I meant everything I said. I wanted everyone within earshot to be inspired, and many people were. That's why I love what I do, but these messages weren't coming from a place of self-awareness. Most of them weren't even original. (There's a whole book titled *N.O.W.* and I didn't write it.) Through Kendrick's music, I noticed that people don't want to be told clichés. They want to hear stories — real, raw, and vulnerable stories they can relate to. They want stories that evoke emotion and stories that remind them of their humanity. Those create lasting impressions. The only anecdotes I was willing to give were stories of success, but we all know life isn't that one-sided.

I learned this for myself when I began to feel like a fraud. I felt like a fraud because I began to realize many around me, even my closest friends, honestly believed my life was perfectly intact. They believed I was always at one hundred percent; they believed I had it all figured out, but none of that was true.

I trip and fall; I feel pain, and I make mistakes just like anyone else. That's what connects us all, and that's what people really want to hear. As I searched for my own authenticity I discovered that any word can momentarily motivate a person, but stories move them. So, I decided I needed to figure out what *my* true story was, and be prepared to share it if I wanted to make the real, long-lasting impact I imagined.

Since freshman year I have been on a personal mission for growth. The Million Man March gave me a million reasons to expand my mind. It's funny how the simplest events in our lives can have the greatest impact. That conversation with Alex was minuscule. I'm sure the others don't even remember having it, but it's one I'll never forget. With this new growth, I have challenged myself to constantly search for truth. Much like K-Dot, I want to be more vulnerable and broadcast my story while remaining my authentic self with everyone I interact with.

However, I learned that before I can accomplish that, I must first be more honest with myself. Learning your history is one of the most powerful gifts you can ever receive. That "history" I speak of can be a variety of things. It can refer to your family history, your personal history, your country's history, your community's history, your culture's history, and anything else that has contributed to who you are or the world you live in.

You know from my introduction that my passion is to help other young people like me and young people like you. Well, Kendrick has another line in "Momma" that I tend to replay in my head. He says, "I know if I'm generous at heart, I don't need recognition... just give it to the kids, don't gossip 'bout how it was distributed."

Consider this conversation as my gift to you. I've always been driven to inspire others, but now I'm driven to inspire others with truth. It took me two decades to find a lot of this wisdom; most of which I found in the past two years alone. With that said, I want to challenge you to find your own truth, whatever that may be.

Question your beliefs to test how much you know about yourself and the world around you because something as simple as one historic event can flip your world upside down.

If this does happen to you, don't be afraid of it because in moments like those, you'll be able to grow the most. You must be willing to question everything and fact check it all. Figure out where it fits into the grand scheme of things. Once you have collected the individual dots, put them together and learn your truth. Then speak it! Since freshman year, I no longer accept everything as fact and neither should you.

THE KENDRICK EFFECT

One of the most salient traits we have as human beings is our vulnerability. But from the surface, that sounds crazy because by definition, being vulnerable means you are opening yourself to attack, either physically or emotionally, and who wants to do that? Why would we willingly decide to expose ourselves or let our guards down... on purpose? If you ask me, I think it's because we are the most truthful when we are vulnerable, and with truth comes connection and understanding. I mean look at me! Here I am immortalizing my vulnerability forever by writing this book. And for what purpose? To better connect and understand you.

Think of the closest friend you have. Notice, I didn't ask you to think about your *best* friend, but I asked you to think of your *closest* friend. For some, that person is one in the same, but for others, these may be separate people. Now think about why that person is your closest friend. Is it because of how cool they are, or because you all can share endless jokes? Or is it because of how *real* they are, or better yet, how much they keep it real with you? We are drawn to those we can trust, and we cannot trust those we do not know.

That's why I trust Kendrick Lamar. I'm not saying Kendrick Lamar is my closest friend—as that would be kinda weird because I've never met the man—but what I am saying is that Kendrick's constant willingness to pour his heart out on wax and be open and vulnerable with, A) Himself and B) His Listeners, has led me to feel as though I can trust him. One of the most powerful songs, to me, on Kendrick Lamar's third studio album, *To Pimp a Butterfly*, is his track "u." In this song, K-Dot talks about his battles with depression, not being there for his loved ones, the struggles that come with fame and riches, and even toying with suicidal thoughts. He put all of this into one song. From my perspective, he created "u" to show how even the strongest figures and greatest leaders are not immune to heartache, depression, or cognitive dissonance.

The year *To Pimp a Butterfly* first came out, I remember watching an MTV interview of Kendrick on YouTube. In the interview, Kendrick said himself that nothing was as vulnerable as "u." He described this record as an expression of him going through change and accepting change. What's funny is that he says accepting change is, "the hardest thing for man to do," and I just told you that being vulnerable is also a very difficult task.

Hmmm, I wonder if there's a connection here. What I appreciated most from this interview was how much I could relate to it. Granted, I'm not a famous rapper on tour (and that's kinda racist if you thought that. Nah I'm just playing!), but I am a first-generation college student away from my family, my homeboys, and the people who count on me the most. One of the biggest strains on Kendrick's mental health, as he puts it, is being on tour while things are going on back home in his city that he "can't do nothing about." This sense of helplessness is something we all go through at some point in our lives. Whether it's having a loved one who's sick, a friend needing emotional support when we're not home, or simply turning on the news to see that there's so much we can't control, Kendrick says that balancing these thoughts can "draw a thin line between having sanity and losing it."

Wow—I want you to let that sink in. The mere thought of all the things we cannot control or fully understand has the potential to make us lose our sanity. I know what you're thinking though, "I'm a teenager, a young adult, and there's no way I can go crazy, right?" Too often when we think about mental health, we don't think about its effects on us as young people. Most of the time we see this as some taboo condition that only affects certain, super depressed kids we know or adults stressing over "life" who drown their sorrows in alcohol. But mental health is a spectrum. It isn't just happy or suicidal; it's everything in between. And as Baltimore poet and youth activist, Kondwani Fidel, once told me, sometimes we are just one traumatic event away from our mental health slipping through our grasp and becoming a person who "wasn't always like that."

What makes this interview with Kendrick so powerful is him displaying that, even as one of the greatest rappers of today and with all his fame and fortune, he is still willing to be vulnerable enough to speak about how this spectrum of mental health has affected him and how he chooses to deal with it. For K-Dot, his release therapy is writing music. And we probably could have guessed that. However, what's more important isn't *what* his release therapy is, but rather *how* he chooses to use it.

Much like you and me, Kendrick views himself as a leader; not as a leader in the traditional sense (even though he clearly is, I mean c'mon it's K-Dot), but as a leader over his experiences. When he made that statement, I realized that's the overarching theme of this interview and of who

Kendrick Lamar is. He takes ownership of sharing his stories, both good and bad, and with his platform as a celebrity he asks himself, "How can I pimp it?" With "it" being his circumstances. He continues, "Can I pimp it negatively, or can I pimp it positively?" In "u" I saw some of the darkest sides of Kendrick come to light.

It really hit home for me when he rapped:

> "What can I blame you for? I can name several situations. I'll start with your little sister bakin'. A baby inside, just a teenager, where was your patience? Where were your antennas? Where was the influence you speak of? You preached in front of 100,000 but never reached her... you f**kin' failure—you ain't no leader!"

This stuck with me on many different levels. I instantly thought about my own little sister. Even though she's seventeen now, I still see nothing but how innocence and sweet and pure she is. All she wants to do is watch her favorite cartoons and play her guitar. She's currently a junior in high school, and I honestly don't know if college is on her radar. Yet, there I was at Georgetown University, and I know college is not the best route for everyone. In fact, it's a huge socially constructed pressure that we place on young people as the end-all, be-all to success (which is a different conversation for a different day), but I can't help but wonder if I didn't do my job as a big brother in empowering my baby sister to know that she deserves to go to the college of her dreams if she wants to.

I also thought about my childhood best friend, Jordan. During my first year in college, I got news that he had gotten caught up in an awful situation and was facing up to ten-plus years in prison for attempted murder. Before the words left the mouth of my friend who was relaying the news, I completely broke down in tears.

"No, no, no, no not J-Whit!" I remember screaming. "This was never supposed to be his lifestyle."

This made me think of another line in "u" when K-Dot says, "A friend never leave Compton for profit." Again, there I was at Georgetown University, struggling with survivor's guilt for deciding to come to this top-tier institution. What was the purpose of me coming here? Was it for the pursuit of a higher education and to learn more about the world? Or was it actually to chase a marketing degree so that I could get a good job and make three times as much as my Nana my first year after graduation? Had I left Charleston for profit?

I also struggled with the fact that I've spoken to and motivated thousands of students and have even been told that I changed some of their lives, yet I couldn't connect with my own sister or change the life of my best friend of twelve years. As a senior in high school, I gave motivational speeches to students about my success as a young entrepreneur and how they too can be empowered to start their own business. Even before then, I was speaking at graduations, sharing my high school experience with middle schoolers, emceeing events all over the city, and constantly sharing my message with whomever I thought needed to hear it. But I was often left to question, "Was any of this worth it if I couldn't inspire the ones who mattered most?"

Thankfully Jordan's case was well resolved and he only had to serve a little over a year in jail, but he's far from the only one. I can easily name at least fifteen friends my age with children, friends who've passed away due to gun violence, and friends who still lead dangerous lives. These are the ones closest to me, who know me best, but who I have the least effect on (or at least that's how it feels).

Your situation doesn't have to be as dramatic as mine to be just as similar. Many of us have that one friend, sibling, cousin, or peer who we wish we could help more. But just because we are unsuccessful with that person doesn't mean we should become mute. If Kendrick never shared his pain in "u" and ultimately in that MTV interview, how would I, or the 1.4 million other viewers on YouTube, be able to use his words as encouragement to continue seeking our own perfect release therapy? Kendrick acknowledges his pitfalls, but he also knows these challenges are worth sharing because we all have a unique story to tell.

Kendrick asks, "How can I be a voice for all these people around the world, but can't reach [my family] like I want to and they're the closest to me. That's a trip."

Yes, it can be a trip, but we all have voices—some filled with pain and others filled with joy—that have a place in the ears and hearts of *someone*. This is what "The Kendrick Effect" is to me. It's being challenged to tell your story and share your truth. For me, Kendrick has affected the way I view vulnerability. I no longer see it as a weakness that needs to be hidden so well, that even I can't tap into it. Instead, I see it as a part of my identity and my past that I must use to shape who I become. Kendrick has also opened my eyes to the power of vulnerability and how it can bring people closer and foster some of the most genuine connections.

THE POWER OF VULNERABILITY

There's a great researcher-storyteller by the name of Brené Brown, who has one of the most powerful TED Talks I've ever seen about vulnerability (FYI: yes, she actually calls herself a "researcher-storyteller"). Brené has spent years studying human connection; she's given a TED Talk, written a book, and even published a theory. As an expert in the field, she says in her speech that, "Connection is why we're here. It's what gives purpose and meaning to our lives." And I couldn't agree more.

Our ability to connect with others isn't just a powerful human characteristic; it's what *makes us* human (have you heard that one before in this book?). This is my third time mentioning this because I think it's something we are often taught to grow out of.

How we perceive the world becomes more and more pessimistic and cold as we get older (some more than others). Think about it; as a child, you hardly ever shy away from telling people exactly how you feel, or from showing your true emotions in front of others. Kids don't wait until they're in the privacy of their own room to cry, nor do they conform to social norms when it comes to opening up and expressing themselves. (BTW: Social norms are the informal rules that a society or community has created and everyone is expected to follow them.) When do we lose that courage? We're constantly told not to talk to strangers (for *very* good reason), not to cry, and to "grow-up." But why does growing up have to mean growing numb?

Brené says that over her six years of research she found that, "When you ask people about love, they tell you about heartbreak. When you ask people about belonging, they'll tell you their most excruciating experiences of being excluded. And when you ask people about connection, the stories they told me were about disconnection."

Ultimately, these negative outlooks boil down to one thing—shame. Brené broke down the word shame in a way that I had never heard before; she said, "Shame is easily understood as the fear of disconnection: Is there something about me that, if other people know it or see it, that I won't be worthy of connection?"

Our shame and *fear of disconnection* leads many of us to never connect with others in the first place. (How backward is that?) Those who have a sense of love and belonging (which we are all entitled to), feel this way because they believe they are *worthy* of that love and belonging. Simple as that. That's the only thing that separates them from those who struggle to grasp this. What's not so simple is building the courage to believe in yourself and to believe in the idea that you are just as worthy of love and belonging as anyone else, even though you are.

After coming to this realization, Brené went on a search. Why were shame and worthiness unraveling connection? Her answer? Vulnerability. A connection cannot arise without it. Brené says, "In order for connection to happen, we have to be seen. Really seen." And there's no way for the world to see you if you have created impenetrable barriers as high as your level of fear and shame.

So, if connection gives our life meaning, and we need to be vulnerable to connect, why do we always view vulnerability as such a cowardly thing? Why aren't more people positively impacted by The Kendrick Effect? After watching Brené's TED Talk, I asked my friends how they would describe vulnerability, and I got responses like "weakness," "giving someone else power," "loss of control," "rare," and "hurt." But I also got back responses like "honesty," "purest form of ourselves," "sacred," and "trusting through the fear." I told you about the Kendrick Lamar interview and how much beauty can come from being open with ourselves and with others. And now here we have an *expert* researcher telling us the same thing! Being vulnerable isn't about doing what's comfortable, or doing what's excruciating… it's about doing what's necessary.

Brené says, "Vulnerability is the core of shame and fear and the struggle for worthiness, but it appears that it is also the birthplace of joy, of creativity, of belonging, of love."

You owe it to yourself not to run away from this powerful force. Are your fears, shamefulness, and worthiness truly good enough reasons to deny yourself the beauty of joy, creativity, and love? I want you to really think about that question because those are all the things you miss out on when you over-guard your heart.

You see, the people who have mastered human connection and belonging have really just built the courage to always show compassion to themselves and to those around them. They also have built the courage to be their authentic selves at all times. This may be one of the most powerful underlying lessons that Brené had to share—being your authentic self requires you to let go of who you think you should be, and just be who you are.

Above all, to be a person who has mastered connection, you must fully embrace vulnerability. That means no more running away from it. No more trying to selectively suppress life's toughest emotions—like vulnerability, fear, anxiety or shame—by getting high, overeating, self-medicating or shopping your way out of it. No more blaming others to hide from your discomfort. No more half-ass steps. From here on out you have to be willing to take leaps of faith and face uncertainty head on. There is no more pretending your actions don't have an effect; take ownership over everything (good and bad) that you do. Follow the ways of K-Dot and Brené and you'll be amazed at how free you will begin to feel.

TAKEAWAYS

Takeaway #1

As youth, sometimes we fail to recognize the importance of certain things in our lives. For example, until we get older, we don't see why we should have eaten our vegetables, or not rushed to be an adult. Discovering your truth, speaking that truth, and being vulnerable with that truth is another one of those strong lessons that's usually overlooked. I told you that being vulnerable is at the basis of our shared humanity, but I never told you why. What separates human beings apart from other species is our self-consciousness.

We know we exist and we know who we are. But with this self-awareness comes the need to have others acknowledge it as well. Nobody wants to go unseen, and vulnerability is the only way to make sure that doesn't happen. It allows us to share our self-awareness with others. It's a process that requires us to have the courage to let our guards down and to recognize, embrace, and empower each other's existence. Sharing our stories, accepting our truths, and exploring our vulnerabilities are the only ways we can continue to be human. And if there's anything you've learned from this chapter, it should be that.

Playing it overly safe with your emotions can be a dangerous habit you begin when you're young. If one of our basic needs is human connection, and you are constantly rejecting the sole ingredient needed for that connection, internal struggle will inevitably follow. It's like those little plastic outlet plugs parents use to protect their babies from getting shocked. There comes a point when that baby should be old enough to manage a wall socket without electrocuting himself. Eventually, that plastic barrier needs to be removed in order for a connection to flow, and for energy to be shared.

Takeaway #2

In addition to recognizing the importance of sharing your story, you should also be aware that being vulnerable isn't only about opening up to what makes you sad; it's also about being truthful with what makes you happy. To me, being vulnerable means being honest. And that means being honest with others, and yourself, about the not-so-good things that may be holding you down. It's about being honest about the pressures or tough memories that may be casting a dark shadow over your life right now. But it's also about being honest and speaking up for the things you believe in. Vulnerability takes being honest in knowing what brings you joy because just as it may take courage to tell your secrets, it also takes courage to tell your passions.

You've probably heard the saying, "The truth hurts," but the truth is also liberating. I just spent a whole chapter encouraging you to find your truth. Even more importantly, I want you to bestow it. Your own personal "truth" can be a lot of different things—you love to cook, you're an agent of social change, music gives you life, or you hope to one day travel the world, etc. Whatever your truth is, don't be afraid to express it in everything you do because that's what will bring you joy. That's the power of vulnerability.

Takeaway #3

Brené shares some great takeaways when it comes to being vulnerable that I think you could learn a lot from too. She breaks them down into four easy parts that may help you visualize what it means to be vulnerable, both with yourself and with other people:

1. **Let ourselves be deeply seen:** This is definitely easier said than done. Essentially, she's urging us to be open enough to allow the outside word to really view who we are. I'll even take this piece of advice a step further and urge you all to also be prepared to deeply *see* others as well because there is nothing more humiliating than building the nerve to open up with someone, just for them to overlook you. If you know what that feels like, you understand the importance in being prepared to help others during vulnerable times.

2. **Love with the whole heart, even with no guarantee:** This seems like a fool's mission, but this is yet another very important piece of wisdom from Brené. There are no guarantees when it comes to love (we'll talk about this more in chapter 3), but in order for love to work, in any situation, you must be bold enough to take that very vulnerable leap of faith.

3. **Practice gratitude and joy, even in moments of terror:** There are going to be times when life seems pretty scary, but embracing those moments will help get you through. Brené says

we must appreciate these moments of extreme vulnerability by acknowledging that, "To feel this vulnerable means I'm alive."

4. **Believe that you are worthy enough:** You ARE worthy of love. You ARE worthy of absolute joy. You ARE worthy of warmth and solace. However, none of these realities will ever matter if you do not believe them to be true yourself. No more of this, "I'm not enough."

Takeaway #4

As I challenge you to be more vulnerable, I encourage you to also be careful with that vulnerability. Just as there are dangers with sharing too little, there are dangers with sharing too much. I've stressed being vulnerable because I honestly believe this is a forgotten trait we as young people have lost touch with. I think our ever-growing digital world has hindered us from achieving the genuine connections we need in our upbringing. However, I also believe that, while we are mindful of this, we must also be aware of who, and who not, to trust with this sensitive information.

There's a reason why so many view vulnerability as a weakness, because in a sense, that's what it is. Yes, this is the only way you can allow yourself to be deeply seen, but it also creates a window of opportunity for your flaws and shortcomings to be exposed. So, while I still ask that you not shy away from telling your story, be sure you're sharing your story with a person or audience you can trust.

I'll wrap up with this, be cautious when it comes to vulnerability, both your own and someone else's. Some things in our lives are private for a reason, but when those conditions start having an effect on your mental health—when it's eating you up or when it begins to cause you stress—that's when having at least *one* person to talk to is necessary.

Odds are, whatever you're experiencing, you're not alone. Finding a friend, a teacher, a counselor, a parent, or a mentor you can open up to is important. You deserve to have people in your life you can trust, and never underestimate the power of your story. If you're bold enough, you may even surprise yourself by how many lives you can impact from sharing your story with complete strangers. Who knows, maybe I'll be reading your book someday!

CHAPTER 2

PIMPIN' THE SYSTEM

—

TRUE STORY #2

The flight attendant had just finished performing the safety instructions, which I always found to be a bit pointless. I remember thinking, "If this plane starts crashing all of that information is going to fly out the window along with our luggage." I chuckled to myself as I made sure to be aware of the closest emergency exit that may be behind me. As she made her way down the aisle, sliding her hands along the railing of the overhead compartments, the pilot's voice rang over the intercom.

"Ladies and gentlemen, we'd like to thank you all for joining us today on our JetBlue flight to Charleston, South

Carolina. The time now is 6:24 p.m....." I tuned him out as I completed my usual takeoff ritual by playing my routine departure song—"Window Seat" by Erykah Badu. As I got comfortable in my chair, somehow the pilot's voice seeped its way back through my noise cancellation headphones, "...In the meantime, please make sure your seat belts are tightly fastened and all electronic devices have been properly stowed away. Once we've reached our maximum altitude of approximately 25,000 feet, I'll turn off your seatbelt signs and you'll be free to roam around the cabin. Again, thank you for flying JetBlue, and enjoy the flight."

I basically knew this whole spiel by heart. I glanced out of the window with hopes that Ms. Badu could calm my nerves. I just wanted a ticket out of town. All I could think about was how rough of a semester I just had that fall. I was beyond ready to leave DC and go home for the winter break. I needed that time to press reset and unwind. As I thought about how tough the tail end of 2017 was for me, I couldn't help but also think about how amazing it was too. At that moment, it dawned on me, *this is the twentieth trip I've taken this year.* You read it right... Two. Zero.

I had traveled 22,732 miles, visited sixteen different cities, taken at least one trip every month, and had done it all over the course of, what was now about to be twenty, separate voyages. But that wasn't even the most astonishing part. What was even crazier was that eleven of those trips were completely free! My excitement didn't stop there, either.

As the landing gear retracted into the belly of the Airbus A320, I did the math and came to realize that for the nine other trips I actually contributed toward, I only spent a little over $2,500 for them in total. That's including travel, food, and some fun attractions (like mountain biking in the Rockies in Denver). $2,500 for a year's worth of traveling? Not bad at all.

Suddenly, 2017 didn't look so gloomy anymore. As my ears popped on a plane for the umpteenth time that year, I couldn't help but ask myself, "Damn, did I really finesse the system like that?" I did more than just finesse it. I pimped the absolute crap out of it! And I hadn't even noticed! Granted, I had to give myself more credit than that. It wasn't as if this was some foreign methodology to me. This was a motto I adopted years ago—right before I began college—once I saw all that I could do with it. Since its adoption, this mindset of always making the best out of every situation transformed from a way of thinking into a way of life over time. I was always finding ways to adapt and adjust, sometimes because I had to and not always because I wanted to. So, it shouldn't have come as such a surprise when I thought back on all that I was able to accomplish that year.

You don't just stumble upon eleven free trips across the Continental US by accident. And you don't just book nine more adventures for a little over $270 each, consequently. This can only be the byproduct of technique and intention, a certain drive and expertise. It takes both time and effort to master the kind of craft that I speak of. Pimpin' ain't easy, but it's also not impossible, and I'll tell you how.

I'm constantly being asked, "Rome, how are you always doing so much and going to so many different places?"

My answer hardly ever changes. Nine times out of ten I'm shrugging my shoulders in response and replying with just four words, "I pimp the system."

This may be a simple response, but it's not that simple of a process. I'm sure by now you are wondering what exactly does it mean to "pimp the system." To be honest, it's an art form that takes refining and practice, but with the right work ethic and intention, it can change your life.

This craft consists of finding loopholes in every metaphorical contract you sign. Whether it's a contract with society, your classes, the government, your scholarships, your job, school, or even your current living situation, micro, opportune moments will always present themselves. And it's up to you to not only to spot these moments as they appear, but also to have the courage to capitalize on them.

Like I said, my year of exploration didn't come about due to chance. In January, my friends and I agreed to sit in on a two-hour info session about Massanutten Ski Resort's new found business of selling condominiums in exchange for a free, two night stay at one of those homes.

Pimped.

In March my scholarship program flew me out to New York City for our annual leadership conference, and I used their resources to fly out to Houston where I spent the rest of my spring break with my best friend, Nick, at his Aunt's house. All I had to pay for was the ticket from H-Town back to Georgetown.

Pimped.

In May, Nick and I decided that we deserved time away from our normal settings, time to explore our creative spirits, and time to see new parts of the countryside. So after our last exam of our sophomore year, he and I took a twenty-four-hour train ride from DC to Chicago, where we stayed with our friend Justus. Then we flew from the Southside to Los Angeles, where I stayed with him for two weeks (Nick's from Watts). During my two-week visit in the Sunny State, our adventurous enthusiasm led us to take a day trip to San Francisco before I flew back to the East Coast to start my internship in New York. My final invoice for this five-city exploration? $470 plus food.

Pimped.

Come August, I would finesse the system like no other. Earlier that year I was accepted into Management Leadership for Tomorrow or MLT (a professional development fellowship for minority students) and my talents also allowed me to receive Intuit's inaugural LIFE Scholarship for STEM and marketing majors. (I just barely made the cut.) Getting these awards wasn't what allowed me to play my cards right, but what I did with them later proved impressive. From August 13 to August 15, Intuit flew me out to San Jose, California, to visit their headquarters and tour the Bay Area (that was my second trip to San Francisco that summer). MLT also had plans of flying me out to Dallas, Texas, for our fellowship's kick-off seminar on August 18.

I realized that left me with a three-day gap in between the two programs. Now, I could've decided to extend my stay in Cali or push forward my arrival in Dallas, but instead, I chose to pimp this to my benefit. I had, essentially, a free trip to and from wherever I wanted to go in the US. So I decided to visit a city I've always wanted to see—Denver, Colorado. I got an AirBnb for $29 a night, went mountain biking on the side of Evergreen Mountain, ate a reindeer hot dog, and tasted some of the best biscuits I've ever had outside of the south. During the month of August, I went from New York to Silicon Valley, Silicon Valley to Denver, Denver to Dallas, Dallas to Charleston, and then from Charleston to DC. And the only flight I paid for was a one-way ticket from Charleston back to DC.

Pimped.

"This is the time to travel and to explore the world. Embrace these next four years, because these will be the best years of your life, and they go by faster than you think." That was one of the greatest pieces of advice I received from a mentor before coming to college.

When I first arrived at Georgetown, I immediately noticed I had a world of new opportunities before me. For the first time in my life, the playing field began to look like it was leveling out. For as long as I can remember, I have been fighting to manipulate a system that seemed to be clearly built against me. As an African-American male, I've had to fight against institutionalized racism, the residual effects of mass incarceration, and countless other forms of systematic oppression. This was finally my time to take from a system that had taken its toll on me for years.

I guess it's safe to say that my hard work, even from before I knew what exactly I was working toward, has paid off. I found myself getting paid to attend one of the best schools in the nation, going to places around the globe this country boy had only dreamed of visiting, and meeting people from worlds so different from my own. If you learn nothing else from this story, I hope you learn this: from here on out, I don't want you to accept any of your circumstances at face value.

If you're currently in a good situation, you should constantly be searching for ways to make it a great one. And if it's a bad situation, you better be on the hunt for a way to flip it around, or at the least, find a way to take something positive from it. No more, "letting the chips fall where they may." You've got to learn how to make the chips fall where you want them!

PIMPIN' THE SYSTEM

This is not a chapter about how to become a millionaire by the time you graduate college. This is a chapter about how to make nearly every situation, every circumstance, every position, and every facet of your life work in your favor. This isn't a collection of secrets designed to prevent you from ever catching a loss again (I catch at least three Ls a week), but rather a compilation of tips on how to finesse bigger wins and transform your losses into something positive.

This chapter is all about finessing the system and making it work for your benefit.

The lesson here isn't for you to find ways to fly all over the country for free or come up with some scheme to collect American Airline reward miles. I recognize I possess a level of privilege in my ability to travel so frequently as a college student. For example, I don't have massive student loans looming over my head (I'll tell you all about that in chapter 6), and I have a best friend who enjoys traveling as much as I do.

However, what you should take away from this chapter is that you are the master of your own abilities. Kendrick's *To Pimp a Butterfly* has taught me that pimpin' is more of a mindset than anything else. In your mind, do you believe you're in control? To master this craft, you need to understand that you control your actions, therefore you control the choices you make, therefore you control your outcomes. Granted, this "control" may only be to a certain extent at times—some things are just truly out of our hands. Nevertheless, no matter how much it may not seem like it, you have to *believe* you are constantly in full rule over your own destiny.

I realize this may seem contradictory, but it isn't. I'll tell you why. Not being in complete control of a certain outcome or happening is a part of life; there will always be other forces at play, some of which you won't be able to wield. You should expect short-term losses to occur from time to time. But, such losses should not matter if your ultimate goal is to win in the long run. Unlike the short-term, what you hope to accomplish in the next three months or the next three years (depending on how long-term we're talking) should always fall within your command because if you have a goal, you should have prepared all the things you need to accomplish it. And if you've done your preparation, you should have a plan of attack to execute all that you've prepared for.

Notice that each step I mention here places the onus on a single person—you. YOU make your own goals. YOU do the prep work. YOU create the strategy. This leaves no room for blame to be placed on anyone but you, and that's how you master the system—by first mastering yourself. In doing so, you're claiming power over every situation. Furthermore, you are putting yourself in a mindset to always win and to always look for new ways to win.

Finessing the proverbial "system" comes about when attitude meets action. Do you have your goals clearly defined? Do you have an idea of how you plan to obtain those goals? Are you constantly aware of favorable circumstances that may help you accomplish those goals? And are you taking a second look at indirect ways for opportunities to assist you with your goals? Because often times our greatest chances to pimp come from opportunities that lie below the surface. The ones everyone else doesn't utilize. The ones everyone else undervalues. The ones everyone else fails to see because their vision doesn't extend as far as yours.

In 2017 I was able to enroll in every class I wanted, secure an amazing internship, and travel all over the country because I had a plan and I stuck to it. I saw opportunity where others didn't. I planned out my vision months in advance. I adapted when my short-term losses set me back. And I didn't waste a second when it came time to capitalize. That year I discovered how to best make the world work in my favor. I traveled. I learned. I grew. I pimped.

THAT "SPARK"

To truly pimp the system takes three things: time, practice, and discipline. It's not something everyone can just do. If it were that easy, more people would be doing it. Executing this type of finesse takes savviness and it takes spunk, both of which aren't developed overnight, but they can be cultivated over time.

My mentor and friend, Jimmy Bailey, has told me the story of how he started Youth Entrepreneurship South Carolina or YESCarolina, a million times, but it wasn't until I interviewed him for this book that I realized the kids in this program have been pimping the system their whole lives. I was once one of those students to go through the YESCarolina Biz-Camp and learned how to be an entrepreneur. What I admire about Jimmy is that he started this nonprofit organization to serve low-income youth because he grew up as a poor kid in Charleston himself. He created YESCarolina because he realized that, "Low-income kids developed a sense of independence and a street sense in order to survive." As Jimmy puts it, these are the kids with the most grit and who have the drive to make something out of nothing. These types of kids know how to finesse, and it's because they treat every situation like their livelihood depends on it. Growing up as one of these kids myself, I can tell you that this type of mentality is a huge part of what it takes to really pimp the system.

As youth today, we have access to all of the world's knowledge at our fingertips. We are seen as the most technologically advanced generation yet, but none of that matters if all we use it for is to take pictures of our food and share an ungodly amount of our lives with the world.

Jimmy told me that no matter how techie young people become, "it's no different today than it was fifty or sixty years ago when [he] was coming up." He then said, "You've got to have the 'spark' that makes you want to learn and you've got to overcome all those things that are in your way."

Do you have that "spark"? When you come across something you don't know, are you curious enough to figure it out? When pieces of the puzzle don't seem to fit, do you feel challenged to make them? Having the drive to learn is the underlying X-factor of pimping the system. Knowledge brings you closer to understanding, and you can't control what you don't know. The more you learn, the more you're able to connect the dots and piece together a world that works to your benefit.

If this isn't the type of person you are currently, don't worry. Youth from low-income households carry this special kind of flame because they have all the motivation they need. However, if you come from a place of privilege, that just means you have to reach a little deeper and figure out what drives you. Then, you'll have to reach deep again and figure out what you want to accomplish. From that point, you can start your journey to learn all you can to help you achieve your goals. Every kid has that "spark" deep inside. The question is, are you motivated enough to tap into it?

BACKED AGAINST THE WALL? BREAK IT DOWN!

Failure can never be an option when you're pimping the system because if you're failing, you're not really pimping. Now, when I say "failure," I'm not talking about the short-term losses I told you to be aware of earlier in this chapter. No one wins all the time. But these setbacks should always be just that—a setback. Remember, the race we're running here is a marathon, not a sprint. I'm not impressed by MC Hammer for making millions just to waste it all. I'm impressed by Jay-Z for making a billion and being nowhere close to done.

I mention Jay because you can only imagine how many times he must've rewritten the rules so he could win a no-win situation. Don't get me wrong, I'm not saying my advice will help you finesse your way to a billion (if it does, I deserve a cut), but I am saying you need this type of mindset. This entire chapter has been about mental discipline. Earlier I told you that if you constantly have your goals top of mind and are consistently on the hunt for ways to accomplish them, you are bound to find the hidden opportunities within every situation. Now I'm telling you to couple that with a mindset of not taking "no" for an answer because then you'll begin to find opportunities that may not have even existed.

I'm not the only one who believes in sometimes flipping the system on its head in order to pimp it. Missy Foy is probably one of the most positive people I've ever encountered. She's the Executive Director of the Georgetown Scholarship Program and she also thinks the system could use some changing. Missy has spent the past ten years assisting and serving low-income, predominately first-generation students at Georgetown University. During her time there she's come to see how access to education can change the lives of so many students who come from underprivileged backgrounds, "and yet, there are still incredible educational inequities and structural barriers to getting a college degree."

When I interviewed her, Missy told me some staggering statistics. She said that if you're born in the bottom percentile, you only have a 9% chance of getting into college.

Meanwhile, those born in the top percentile, have a 77% chance of getting a higher education.

"It's inexcusable, as a society, that where you happen to be born, what zip code you're born into, can determine your fate. That's crazy!"

This is a reality for students across the country. I believe, and Missy would agree with me, that we as a society place too much of the onus on students as a way of deflecting our institutional problems (if this is going over your head right now, you're welcome. This will give you something to Google). Granted, I did tell you that the onus falls on us when it comes to our goals, but it shouldn't fall on our shoulders when it comes to educational inequality.

Missy also told me, "The narrative right now is that the student just needs to better learn to navigate the system."

I saw a sarcastic smirk smear her face, "I wish the conversation was why isn't the system changing?"

Missy was more than likely asking this question rhetorically, but I believe I have an answer for it. There's no change happening because, for many folks, "the system" isn't broken. And we all know the saying, "If it ain't broke, don't fix it."

Well, I got a couple sayings in response to that.

"If your back is against the wall… BREAK DOWN THE WALL!"

"If you don't like how the table is set… FLIP OVER THE TABLE!"

And, "If the system's broken… PIMP IT!"

TAKEAWAYS

Takeaway #1

We've talked about a lot of things in this chapter. I told you how pimping the system isn't a deceptive process but a strategic one. I also told you how it's more of a mental thing than anything else. It's how you view the world around you. Do you see opportunities that others don't? Can you bounce back from small Ls to catch the big Ws? Are you determined to be vigilant about what you want? Do have that "spark" that makes you want to learn? And are you prepared to bust through whatever barrier may stand in your way?

These different components are needed to put yourself on a self-constructed pathway toward success; versus relying on the universe to get it done for you. However, before any of these pieces can complete the puzzle, one thing has to be at the center of it all—your goals.

Without your goals, you have nothing to work toward. How can you finesse a situation if you don't know what you are finessing it for? Don't underestimate how much guidance you can get from having your goals in front of you. You will quickly learn that your goals are the driving catalyst behind how you navigate the opportunities before you.

Takeaway #2

Once you've written down your goals, you need to strategize how you're going to accomplish them. The second biggest takeaway from this chapter is how are you preparing yourself for success? This includes taking the time to have coffee chats with folks during your internship, asking a friend to keep you accountable, creating a schedule and sticking to it, and reminding yourself of your goals every day. If you're always prepared, you never have to get ready. And you can't pimp a situation if you're not ready. Otherwise, that opportunity will just past you by.

One of my mentors would call this, "putting yourself in the path of luck." Are you setting yourself up so that when a once-in-a-lifetime opportunity presents itself, you'll be able to say yes?

Takeaway #3

The final takeaway is straightforward. Learn how to adapt. A part of being young is being resilient. And your bounce-back game has to be strong to pimp the system. Ls are inevitable. The question is, how are you going to grow from them and make something positive? This is where that "mindset" I've been talking about comes into play.

Be aware that adapting isn't just rearranging the plans when things go bad, but also being ready to shift gears when unexpected triumphs occur too. That's ultimately how you finesse. Can you switch up things for the better and keep pushing forward?

CHAPTER 3

LOVE IS LOVE

——

TRUE STORY #3

I've had to come to terms with love and all of its ugly beauty on my own. To be honest, I still haven't completely figured it out yet, and I'm not sure if I ever will. My mother had me when she was nineteen years old. I can only imagine how scared and uncertain about the future she must've been at that age. But you know what? She always found a way to make everything work, as most strong, black mothers do. Although, "making it work" came with a hefty toll sometimes.

My mom was first arrested for writing fraudulent checks when I was about three years old. I'm certain she did this with good intentions of trying to provide a better life for me and herself, but unfortunately, that wouldn't be the last time. Around this age my grandparents on my mom's side took me under their care, and they would raise me (for the most part) as my mom struggled with the judicial system for the next twelve years or so. Most of my childhood after that point would prove to be a constant uphill battle against resentment, abandonment, and trust. My parents quickly found themselves in the business of buying expensive things with fraudulent checks and then selling them for profit or returning them to the stores they purchased them from for cash. They also would come to engage in a variety of different illegal activities, but this was their crime of choice.

No matter how much they covered their tracks, improved their methods, or switched their guinea pigs, the North Charleston Police Department would always catch up to them in the end (sounds kinda stupid to continue doing the same thing, doesn't it? I thought so too, even as a kid). The result? I went years without having a mother. Approximately five to be exact—give or take a few months. But these five years wouldn't be just one long sentencing; it was a compilation of missteps, poor judgment, and heartbreaking arrests that stretched over the course of fifteen years of my life. By the time I was a freshman in high school, my mom had missed a third of my upbringing and by that point, I hated her for that. I sometimes wondered if I would have felt the same if she served her time consecutively instead of dragging the time out over the duration of my childhood. Every new arrest reopened the most painful chest wound I've ever experienced, and it would happen so frequently that this wound took ages to heal.

Too many times I've had to bear witness to a sight no child should ever see. I've seen my mom, the woman I love the most, put in handcuffs at least three times in my life. The first time I saw this with my own eyes was in third grade. I was coming home from school. I had just gotten off the school bus and I turned the corner to go down my street, just to find a line of police cars outside of my home. I remember being scared, but not confused.

I saw my front door completely demolished. What once kept the dangers of the world out and the ones I loved in was now a pile of wood chips on my welcome mat. I saw detectives with their thin police boomers and exposed badges on their hips like in the movies. I saw officers remove all of our belongings. I saw my neighbors step out of their houses to look at us with eyes of shock and disappointment (my friend across the street never hung out with me again after that day; in fact, his mom wouldn't even let him open the door when I knocked). And I saw my mama in the backseat of a squad car.

There were tears running down her face. There were even more running down mine. While her tears were filled with shame, mine were filled with fear. I remember asking myself, "What are they going to do with her?" I had no idea what was going to happen next. All I knew was that I missed her already; she didn't deserve what was happening to her, and I couldn't wait to hug her again.

I went eight months without that hug. Instead, we were forced to exchange our love through letters, our laughs via phone, and our kisses through glass. In my early years, it drove me crazy not being able to see my mom whenever I wanted, so I made a constant effort to gain contact with her any way I could. I was her baby boy, and she had my nickname of "Fat Boy" tattooed on the scroll that went across the teddy bear on her upper left shoulder.

I felt like she always needed me. That symbolic teddy bear wears combat boots and is dressed in military clothing. As a kid, I internalized that as her needing me to be her soldier at all times; ironically, one of her favorite songs when I was growing up was "Solider" by Destiny's Child. My younger self saw my mom as more than just my mother, but as a queen whose honor needed to be defended and protected.

So that's exactly what I did. I fought for my mama by staying strong for my younger brother and sister and comforting them with the same lies of extended "work trips" that were once told to me. I also went to battle for my mama by combating my own grandparents when they would talk negatively about her parenting abilities in front of me. But my deadliest attacks came in the classroom. I would bust my ass in school with the hopes that it would make my mom proud enough to encourage her to stay home and to let her know she didn't have to keep breaking the law to make our lives better. I was fine with the food stamps, the rusty car, the Section 8 housing, and even a few roaches if it meant we were all together, but that was a battle I always lost.

Over time, my eagerness and childlike passion to stay connected with my mother slowly faded, and resentment began to take its place. If I had a therapist, he would probably say I began to struggle with abandonment issues. Having her taken away from me ripped my heart out of my chest every time, and only the warmth and fullness of her presence and loving grip could sew me back together. But this wasn't a game of Operation. She couldn't just keep doing this to me and expect me to have the same foolish smile every time she returned. And if this was the board game of Operation, her hand became less and less careful as she placed my heart back into place. Each selfish mistake would send a new, piercing pain through my rib cage, worse than the one before.

———

I'll never forget coming home to my grandparents' house one day after school when I was in the fourth grade to find my mama sitting on the couch. I was ecstatic! I couldn't believe my eyes! There was nothing that could have made me happier. I jumped on her and squeezed her and overpowered her with my love. I felt a lump build at the base of my throat; it was impossible to swallow. I couldn't say a word. There was nothing but joy running down my cheeks and that same joy stained her stomach. Her warm palm cradled my chubby jaw and her soft lips kissed my scruffy hairline. I wrapped my arms around her waist and was able to lock my fingers just enough to never let her go.

She had been home for a few weeks or so I believe when one day she offered to walk me to school (it was only a five-minute walk that I normally took by myself), but I guess there was something special about that day. I remember that morning like it was yesterday. It was cool and foggy outside, the type of weather that creates perfect drops of dew on each blade of grass. I enjoyed that kind of weather though. I would always do the weirdest things with my mouth when it was just cold enough because I could see my breath. It never took much to amuse me. I was so fascinated by the miniature clouds leaving my lips that I didn't pay much attention during our walk. I wish I had.

My mom walked me to the patch of grass that separated my school from our neighborhood. She never brought me to the front door. She'd been gone so long, and the school probably wouldn't have known who she was. I was ready to finish my walk to school on my own (the strawberry milk was always the first to go), but she didn't let go of my hand. She pulled me to her then gave me a kiss and a hug that was a little longer and little warmer than usual. When she finally let me go, I looked back to see only her silhouette through the fog. It wasn't long before I couldn't see her at all. She was gone.

I came home from school that day excited to share with my mom what I learned. When I walked through the door, I was met by Nana sitting on the couch.

I asked her, "Where's mama? I gotta show her something!"

She looked back at me with eyes full of sorrow. "They came and got her earlier today, Boogie."

I froze. I didn't even have the urge to cry. I felt broken. How could she be gone already? I just got her back. God,

I hated "them." I knew exactly who "they" were before my grandmother could even finish her sentence. "They" always broke up my home with their battering rams. "They" never let me have her when I needed her the most. "They" made sure my heart weighed a thousand pounds. But, I was aware it was ultimately her fault why "they" continued to come. She forced their hand and she made her own bed.

I used to think she wrote those checks for us—me, Danjai, and Darius—but the evidence proved otherwise. For all I knew, she wanted to leave. She obviously didn't want to be here, because if she did, she would've been. That day my pain turned into hatred. My heart, instead of breaking, froze over. I grew cold.

I was a kid, but even in my innocence, I knew I couldn't handle this kind of emotional suffering much longer. As much as I didn't want to admit it, the real source of my heartache was my mama. So, in fourth grade, I decided I wasn't going to let myself get attached to her, or anyone for that matter, any more. I figured if I didn't care when she was home, I wouldn't care when she wasn't, and vice versa. As harsh as it may sound, I got used to not having a mother.

———

From early 2009 to late 2011—about two and a half years—she would serve her last and longest sentencing yet. During that time, she missed some of my greatest personal achievements, but I didn't care. Her letters didn't get a response; her calls didn't get an answer, and she didn't get a visit from me. I had washed my hands of her.

I hated her for not being there to see me grow. I hated her for putting the burden of raising her kids on Nana. I hated her for always putting her partner in crime (her husband) before us. I hated her for making my little brother and sister go through the same pain I went through. I hated her for monopolizing all of my tears. I hated her for always saying sorry but never meaning it. And I hated her for making me love her so much.

Saying that I carried a heavy heart those two years would be an understatement. Even with the front I tried to put up, even with the smile I never let fade, depression always lingered. I missed her. I missed telling her I missed her.

Those two years took a toll on me, but I never let it distract me. She would surprise me in my memories from time to time, but I was always immediately reminded of the pain. I never felt like I had someone I could talk to about these feelings. So I treated my head like an

Etch-A-Sketch pad and would shake until those memories were gone.

I clearly didn't know how to handle the conflicting emotions of love and anger that were at war in my soul. Up until I was fifteen years old, I played a tormented game of cat and mouse with her. I had just begun my freshman year when the umpteenth round of this game we played was approaching. She was scheduled to be released soon, and a celebration I used to look forward to more than Christmas had become just another day for me. Ever since that dreadful day in fourth grade, I always tried to act mad whenever she returned, but her grace and unconditional love were so infectious that the tough guy routine wouldn't last longer than twenty-four hours. But this time was different. I was much older now, and I wasn't acting anymore.

I burst through the front door of our apartment, like I did every day after school, and let out an obnoxiously loud, "Naanaaaaaaa! Where ya' at ole girl?" As the man of the house, this was my usual, "Honey, I'm home," announcement.

"I'm in the kitchen, boy!"

"Haha, what you cooki—" I instantly saw *her* from the living room. There she was sitting at the dining room table with a small grin on her face.

"What? Cat got your tongue?" If you left it up to Nana, she'd swear she was a comedian.

It wasn't just a cat; it was a raging lion. I wasn't prepared for *her* to be home that day. I mean, I knew she was supposed to be back soon, but I guess amidst my lack of caring, I lost track of time. With wide arms, she stood up to give me a hug.

"Hey, Boogie!"

"Hey, Mama..." With one arm, I hugged her back. There was no joy running down my cheeks this time—just a stale face.

My two years of pent-up resentment and apathy were more than apparent. I didn't know how I felt about her return, so I did what I do best and chose not to feel at all. This neutral numbness was all I had to offer. She had been gone for so long. How was I supposed to feel?

My detachment lasted for weeks. I tried my hardest to avoid her, but she was relentless. She couldn't break me this time around though; I wouldn't let her. In my eyes, she had a lot to prove before she could get anything out of me. I didn't have the slightest urge to talk to her about anything. But in my heart I knew my expectations for her to earn my trust back were unreasonable requests. If anything, I wanted them to be impossible for her to meet because I was scared to let her back in. Could you blame me?

———

Weeks went by after her release and I still didn't know how to cope with it all. I wanted every reason to be mad at her. Hell, I *had* every reason to be mad her. But, carrying so much animosity and bitterness began to take just as much energy out of me as caring and being hurt. It was like I couldn't win for losing.

My friend Keenan was the first to talk to me about this weight on my heart. We were hanging out in my room one day after school when he asked me, "You happy to have your mama back home?"

I sighed as I looked down at the carpet. "Honestly, I don't know how to feel, bruh."

He was puzzled. "What you mean?"

"She always does this shit, man. One day she home. One day she locked up. I'm tired of playing this game with her. Between you and me, I haven't really talked to her since she's been home."

"Dang, that's crazy. I feel you bro, but at the end of the day, that's still your mama."

He was right. She was still my mom. I had no choice but to love her, or at the very least, forgive her. Otherwise, that hatred was going to eat me alive. It took real effort to carry such a grudge. That was when I learned that hate is not the direct opposite of love. They actually share a lot in common. Both emotions require intense passion, and they both are forms of immense affection (one negative, one positive). Hatred, in its own right, is rooted in love. What I discovered was that the true opposite of love is dismissiveness. When you no longer feel anything toward a person is when you can claim to no longer love that person. I wasn't heartless. I still cared for her, and I didn't have it in me to become fully indifferent toward my own mother. So for the sake of my own mental health, I knew I needed to forgive her.

This didn't prove to be an easy process, but it started with communication. Once I got myself to have a conversation with her that was more than just "How was your day?" and "Good," I was able to let my guard down more and more. Even with all the pain she caused me in the past still at the back of my mind, I found a way to smile at the fact that I had her in the present. Not to be mistaken, just as this process wasn't easy, it wasn't quick either. It took me more than two months before I felt comfortable enough to even share a genuine laugh with her, but slowly we got there.

I'm sure it must've hurt when I avoided her countless efforts to contact me while she was away. I still feel slightly guilty for being so selfish, but I'm almost certain nothing hurt more than when she came home to the same treatment in person, when she realized that this wasn't just some phase, when she realized I was for real. I have to admit that I admired her patience and willingness to let me come back to her on my own terms. She waited for me for over a year with the same wide arms that I wasn't ready to embrace that day in the dining room. She was relentless. After a prolonged time of self-reflection, healing, and baby steps, my heart was finally ready to re-accept her love and forgive her wholeheartedly.

As soon as I decided to bury the hatchet, warmth returned to her hugs and a joyful cadence returned to her voice. I felt like I had a mom again.

Those years I went without her shaped my view on love and attachment. Two sentiments that should go hand in hand became separate feelings for me. I would love but not get attached to some. And I would grow close, but never actually love others. It's safe to say that those years without her shaped how I go about accepting and expressing love to this day. It definitely shaped my relationship with her forever, and it shaped how I approach every other relationship since.

If there's one thing I learned from all of this, it's that there's no room for pride when it comes to love. Being open enough to love someone—whether that's your mom, your friend, your cousin, your partner, your sibling, your whoever—takes an immense amount of vulnerability and cooperation. Both of which have no constructive use for arrogance and stubbornness. So yes, the connection my mom and I have may never be the same as a mother and son who didn't have to endure what we did. However, what we have is still rich with love, it's healthy, and it brings me joy.

Building the moral courage to forgive her prepared me for what was to come later in my life. That year she came home was the same year my Papa left my Nana after being with her for thirty-five years. He was the only father figure I ever knew, and he decided to disappear during the most formative years when a boy becomes a man. He just left with no warning. My Papa taught me nearly everything I knew. So to see him leave was like seeing a part of me go with him. I thought I would lose my grandfather to natural causes, not to a homewrecker. With him gone, I was forced to grow up quicker than I should have.

Nevertheless, forgiving my mama helped me when I eventually had to forgive my grandfather for leaving our family to be with another. It's ironic because he used to constantly say, "The kids always come first," whenever he would criticize my mom's poor parenting habits. Yet, there he was doing the same thing she used to do, leaving. I still took his advice, though, and I put the kids (myself) first. So I forgave him, just like how I forgave my mom, for the reason to improve my own self.

It's safe to say that my childhood was a rollercoaster of emotions and hardships. But it was grounded in life lessons and love. Even though she was gone for a third of it, there was never a part of my upbringing that I didn't feel loved by my mother. I knew she thought about me every time she saw that teddy bear on her arm. I knew she was praying for me because God seemed to answer all her prayers. And I knew she missed me because her letters only grew longer as her time away went on.

I have a cousin who stole my very first iPod when I was twelve. I have another one who robbed my mama's house when I was sixteen. I have a father who has never made an effort to connect with me. I have an aunt who was willing to let me go into child protective services. I have a grandfather who I admired more than anyone who left me. And I have a mother who... well, you know that story. At the end of the day, all of these people, with all of their flaws, are still my family. No one comes from a perfect home, and I'm a strong believer in something my Papa always told me, "You ain't gotta like 'em, but you gotta love 'em." That ideology has led me to forgive each of them because family is family and love is love.

LOVE IS LOVE

Love has chewed me up like cheap steak and spat me out like spoiled milk. Love has left me in shambles. Lost. And very much confused. Ironically, at the same time, love has also given me some of the most joy of my life. Love has provided me with solace and a place to rest my heart when the world seems to be a bit too much for me to bear alone. This abstract concept has led me to resent it and embrace it all at the same time. How crazy is that? I mean seriously, that's some extreme cognitive dissonance happening. Yet, here I am. (I realize I say that a lot in this book—"yet here I am." I promise I'm not trying to be corny. I think it's more so a self-reflection of how far I've come.)

I honestly feel, as young people, we are told all the time that "we're too young to know anything about love." And even though there is some truth to that, I believe that's Bullshit.

(Yes, I said "Bullshit," but Bullshit with a capital *B* is actually a philosophical term—trust me, I learned it in college.) Think about that, though. Who is society to tell us that we don't know anything about love? If anything, as youths, we express the most, authentic forms of love. Our love is the most unconditional *because* of how little we've been exposed to the evils of the world. Our innocence, or at least our perceived innocence, is why the world tries so hard to protect young people. Because our love is pure. Because our love is whole. And because our love is blind.

Believe me when I tell you this, that warm fuzzy feeling you have in the pit of your gut when you're twelve and you're finally about to kiss that one person you've had a crush on since sixth grade is the same fuzzy feeling you get when you're twenty-two and that special person finally gives you the shot you've been waiting on since freshman year of college. (Random Lesson: ALWAYS shoot your shot, young blood! Otherwise you'll never be in the game.) And the same applies when you're thirty-two, forty-two, fifty-two, you name it!

My Nana is sixty-two and just recently reconnected with an old lover who she hasn't heard from in over forty years. They found each other on Facebook and slowly began talking to each other again. She's in South Carolina and he's in Florida, but they now speak to each other for hours on end, every day of the week. She even pretends to like football so that they can chat on Sundays while watching the game together. The point here is that every time she talks about him, I see the same spark in her eyes as a high school girl falling for the cute boy. My Nana describes it as a "daydream" she never expected. I say this to make the claim that the way we feel emotions doesn't change. However, the way we understand them matures over time.

With that said, I believe you do know what love is. You know what it's like to have a crush; what it's like to love your family; what it's like to love your closest friends, and what it's like to have a passion. Sure, you may not know what it's like to be *in* love with someone romantically because you haven't experienced enough to know what that is like, but you do know how love feels and how it feels to love something or someone. However, dealing with that strong and powerful emotion (in any capacity) can be difficult for us at times. This is where our lack of experience and exposure hinder us. Time has a funny way of working with life to teach us most things. Unfortunately, these are normally not resources we have at our disposal when we're young. I hope this chapter can supplement some of that void for you.

ACCEPTING & EXPRESSING LOVE

How many of you have had the benefit of having at least one person in your life shower you with love? For me, I'd have to say that person is my Nana. She's the one person that's been there for me through thick and thin. She's never left my side, physically or emotionally. I honestly don't give her enough credit, but my grandmother has always been my number one fan, my PR person, my travel agent, my secretary, and my overall biggest supporter. Don't get me wrong, my mom, grandpa, and countless other family members have showered me with love too, but in hindsight, my Nana has been there since day one (she's the real MVP!).

It's easy for me to envision myself showering my future children and grandchildren with the same amount of love because of how much I've received. However, I can't imagine me having that same outlook if I didn't know what it felt like to accept and express love at all.

My friend, Allison Hilton, encounters kids all the time who don't know what love is. She currently works with three to four-year-olds (preschoolers), but has also worked with middle schoolers and students from the ages of fourteen to twenty-one during her time as Assistant Director of the After School Kids Program in Washington, DC. Across the board, Allison says that she has witnessed young people in desperate need of love—in need of knowing how to:

1. Express love

2. Receive love

"Jerome, I'm not gonna lie to you; it's the absolute most heartbreaking thing when you realize that a child has not been loved." Allison also told me, "Just as a human being" so many kids do not hear, "I love you and respect that you are here and think that you deserve dignity."

While she was still with the ASK Program, she remembers working with one student who was just about to turn eighteen years old. The program decided to take the youth group up to the mountains for a trip to get them out of the city. Amidst their trip, there was time for reflection.

This was a trip filled with bonding between the mentors and the participants. As they appreciated the nature around them, as well as the company they shared, this particular student told Allison, "Y'all are the only people who've ever told me you love me..."

Allison responded by asking, "You're eighteen years old. What do you mean?"

"Before you said it, nobody else had ever said it to me."

Can you imagine being in his shoes? How about experiencing nearly eighteen years of life and never hearing the words "I love you" directed toward you personally? My Nana would tell me she loved me nearly every day and I remember, embarrassingly, having to say it back in front of my friends in elementary school as I tried to quickly whip her lipstick off my cheek. I may have been annoyed, but I knew I was loved. Looking back on it, I realize how ungrateful I would have looked in the eyes of the young man that broke Allison's heart that day. It's amazing how much we take for granted, especially something as ubiquitous as love.

This young man in particular was an "at-risk" (I quote this term because I don't completely agree with its definition, but I believe its the best descriptor in our current society) youth who had gotten several gun charges, committed robberies, lost friends to gun violence, and was literally living to survive. There's no telling what the power of love could have done to change his trajectory. Yet there he was—eighteen and unloved.

But not just teenagers experience this deprivation of love. Allison says she's witnessed this among her preschoolers too. As the Students and Support Specialist at Mitchell

Elementary School in Charleston, South Carolina, Allison found herself working with a young person who was four years old, and who didn't initially know what to do when she gave him hugs or even just showed kindness toward him. This was a foreign emotion to him. He would look at her with funny, analytical eyes of confusion. These interactions were so strange to him that he didn't know exactly how to respond when her arms covered him with warmth and security.

Over time, he began to not only accept these acts of kindness, he embraced them. He sought them out. He needed them.

Unfortunately, Allison said it eventually "got to the point that, when I walked I'd tell him good morning, give him a hug, and get him ready for the day. Then when another student would come in and I would hug him too, he would lash out at me because I was showing love to someone else."

Not only did he not know how to accept love, he also didn't know how limitless love can be. How transferrable it truly is. Or as Allison puts it, he didn't know that "love can be spread to more than one person." She realized he felt that way because "he doesn't see love on a consistent basis."

Allison's story is worth sharing because it shows how we, as young people, can be forgotten about. Love is such a universal thing; it's strange to think that there are kids out there without it. And if you feel as though you are one of those kids, I want you to know that there is no greater force than the love that you have for yourself. You see, there's no one in this world who is obligated to love you except for you.

With that said, I challenge you to say, "I love myself," and mean it. The day these three words hold truth will be the day you'll never be alone because with self-love comes inner happiness, personal affection for who you are, and peace of mind. I'm not saying that, by simply loving himself, the teenage boy in the ASK program would have magically had a better life, but I am saying there should never be a time when you feel as though no one loves you because you should always love yourself. Again, to be fair, what I'm saying is easier said than done, but it's necessary.

I'm preaching self-love here because I remember those times when I felt deprived of my mother's love. Much like the four-year-old boy Allison works with, I forgot how to accept love from others. Actually, I taught myself not to accept or express love to guard myself from being hurt by it again. As a result, I found myself struggling to be happy with who I am because not only did I hide my true emotions from others, I hid them from myself.

So when it comes to expressing love, accepting love, and feeling loved, I believe spreading this powerful emotion within yourself is the best form of practice. By expressing love to yourself, you're accepting it, and by accepting this love you get to feel it. This type of "love-training" exercise is invaluable because when it comes time for you to do this with others, you'll be an expert. I'm a firm believer that you can't truly love someone else until you've learned how to love yourself.

TAKEAWAYS

Takeaway #1

The first thing you should take away from this chapter is this: Learn how to forgive and re-open your heart.

I feel as though embracing forgiveness is a hard thing for us as young people to do. To be honest, it's a hard thing for anyone to do. Much like the stigmas surrounding vulnerability, forgiveness is another one of those traits that people tend to associate with weakness as if forgiving means granting power. Choosing whether or not to forgive someone has nothing to do with that other person and everything to do with you. It is impossible to lead a life of happiness with hatred in your heart. Regardless if you've got a beef with an old friend, a teammate did you wrong, or an ex cheated on you, if you don't find it in your heart to forgive that person, that bitterness will slowly deteriorate your peace of mind while that person continues to live their best life.

I guess there is some sort of granting of power happening when you decide to forgive, but it's not from you to another. Instead, it's for you to yourself. Through forgiveness, you grant permission to rid yourself of the pain and distress. You give yourself back that power over your emotions and your life.

You will love plenty of individuals who will slight you in some way, shape, or form. It may be minuscule or it may be life changing. The size of his or her breach of trust will determine whether you allow that person back into your life or not, but no matter the circumstance, forgiveness toward that person is a must. It is the only way to internally liberate yourself from any toxic situation.

But to be clear, forgiving is not forgetting. You would be a fool if you thought those two things were synonyms. This is where folks begin to associate weakness with forgiveness because some people will forgive *and* forget. Malicious people in your life will take your amnesia and use it as a pass to repeat their offenses. I forgave my mom, but I never forgot what she did to me. And I made sure she knew that I would never forget. Even though I treated her harshly, maybe she needed that tough love because she hasn't seen the back of a squad car since.

The lesson I'm trying to teach here is to be mindful of your relationships with people. Always self-assess how you are treating them and how they are treating you. Most of all, you must be selfish when it comes to your happiness and your levels of emotional currency (the amount of emotional "dollars" you have to spent). As strange as it may sound, sometimes forgiving others is the best way to put yourself first.

Takeaway #2

Though forgiving is important, loving yourself is ten times more valuable! Here are some easy first steps you can begin to take to start fostering the love you need to have for yourself.

1. Think about the traits you enjoy the most about yourself and embrace those every day. (This includes gassing yourself about how cute you are—Recommended Location: Bathroom Mirror.)

2. Remind yourself of your strengths every day. Although your strengths may overlap with your traits, they are not one and the same. Traits are the patterns of your characteristics that make you who you are—i.e., your goofiness, your infectious smile, or that weird thing you do whenever you see your best friend in the hall. Meanwhile, your strengths are the powerful personality advantages you possess—i.e., your positive outlook or your communication skills.

3. Surprise yourself with your favorite things from time to time, no matter how small. This could be ice cream, a haircut, watching your favorite movie, a bike ride, getting your nails done, whatever!

4. This is the most important, yet simplest, step of them all. Constantly say out loud, "I love myself." (Go ahead, do it right now!) Even if you don't believe this to be true now, you'll be surprised at how quickly you'll begin to internalize this. But the trick is to say it out loud because then the message is relayed three times—you thought it, you said it, and you heard yourself say it. Then soon you'll believe it.

CHAPTER 4

LOST IN THE SAUCE

———

TRUE STORY #4

"If a man does not have sauce, then he is lost. But the same man can be lost in the sauce."

— GUCCI MANE

Do you have sauce? Are you lost in that sauce? This was one of the funniest quotes I've ever heard from Gucci. If it were ever to be taught in an academic setting, it would most likely fall under the Hood Philosophy department. But through the laughter, I felt as though Gucci's words had quite a bit of truth to them.

All jokes aside, *have* you ever felt lost? Or scared out of your mind by the simple *idea* of even being lost?

Well, I have. To be a hundred with you, I feel lost right now. In this very moment. As I type these words on this page.

According to Google being "lost" means that you are unable to find your way—unknowing of your whereabouts. For me, I haven't been feeling "lost" in a physical sense. I know where I am. I know how to get home from this coffee shop on M Street and which direction will take me there. Yet, here I am, lost as shit. Mentally—lost as shit. And I've been feeling this way for quite some time now.

I don't know about you, but I am constantly in need of my own personal roadmap in my head that keeps me on track. It's a map filled with ideas, decisions, and most of all, directions. I use this mental roadmap of mine to judge how much time I should spend working on an assignment, and then I determine how much time I'll need for my plan B when I inevitably decide to procrastinate (seriously, I do not know how this book got finished). This roadmap lets me know who I can trust with my feelings. It tells me who and where to invest my love. My psychological map reminds me of who I am and what my best interests are. I then, in turn, use this moral compass to make the best decisions that will help me achieve my goals.

As crazy as this may sound, I feel like Dora the Explorer every day I wake up. Not in the gist of me believing that I am a small, Mexican girl, but in the same sense of how Dora depended on her trusted map before she went on *any* journey with Boots. However, unlike Dora, as I begin my new journey every day, I've been searching in my purple backpack and have found nothing but lint. My map is gone.

What's worse is that the road I've been forced to continue traveling down (because usually life doesn't allow us to stop for breaks) is starting to look fuzzy. It's like traveling on a new highway, going sixty-five miles per hour (because you gotta keep up with the traffic), with no GPS, and then it begins to rain so hard that you can't even see the lines on the road that are directly in front of you, yet you're still expected to drive.

That's how lost I feel.

What's most frustrating is that I feel like I know where my internal misdirection is coming from. For starters, I'm the slowest writer I know and I'm writing a book! Not to mention, I constantly feel this moral obligation to give. This responsibility stems from me recognizing that I am a Black man who has achieved a level of "success" that many of peers have not. I give everything that I have—my energy, my time, my compassion, my happiness—to help others. Especially others who look like me, talk like me, and remind me all too much of myself.

Add in the school work of a university that I was never prepared for, and you have one very overwhelmed college student. I told you in my introduction that college was when I almost drowned. Well, I feel my iceberg is approaching. The weird thing is, I'm not doing poorly in my classes. My GPA is decent. I have an internship offer for the summer. I'm starting my own company. I'm doing everything (and then some) that I'm supposed to. But still, I feel lost, and much like a kid who wondered away from his parents in Walmart and finds himself scared in the middle of an aisle. Sometimes you just can't pinpoint where exactly you took the wrong turn.

We both know more than just school can cause us stress. We are easily overwhelmed by our parents, our passions, our college searches, our job searches, our friends, and those who we wish were more than friends. I told someone really close to me a few months ago that I had feelings for her, and she hasn't made it clear if she feels the same (yeah I know, deep in the friend zone and I caught feels).

Based off her words, there's hope. However, based off her actions, I feel like she's just searching for the right way to let me down easily. Since the day I told her, our relationship has become murky. It has left me to wonder if my hopes of seeing us together, and rolling those dice, was ever worth this nightmare of losing our friendship. Regardless, her intentional, ambiguous, and delayed response has only added to my inner confusion. (I can't believe that I'm writing about her. I wonder if she'll ever read this.)

Yet, feeling lost doesn't stop there either. Lostness is closely correlated with loneliness. Trust me, I've been there before too. I know for me, I am surrounded by nothing but great friends and a support system filled with folks who are rooting for me—some are folks that I don't even know personally. But in times like these, I still feel alone. Loneliness is one of those interesting concepts because just like lostness or depression, it can hit you out of nowhere. And I mean *nowhere.* You can be the most popular person and still feel alone.

Currently, the girl I thought I wanted the most is avoiding me, I'm questioning who I am, and I feel like I don't have a genuine connection to anyone. Except for one person, my best friend, Nick. But that is far from healthy. Remember when I said that vulnerability is one of the most salient traits we have as human beings? This trait is important because it is the gateway to human connection. Without that you can find yourself lost and lonely, which is a pretty sucky combination.

You may have experienced this too, but not having a genuine connection with anyone makes me feel fake. I'm going to parties I don't enjoy and cracking jokes I don't find funny. When people ask me how I'm doing, I smile and say I'm fine because I feel like I have to. I'm Romey Rome. Sweet, loving, motivating, Romey Rome. How could I afford not to be okay? How can I claim to be a motivational speaker if I can't motivate those around me?

And for those who know me well enough to ask me what's really going on, I lie by placing blame on my school work and the stress of everything that's "Georgetown" related. (I put Georgetown in quotes because, at a top-tier university like this, it is easy to find yourself caught up in the sleepless, competitive, frenzy that often swarms this campus.)

But it's more than that. There's an indescribable hurt on the left side of my chest that I have no way of putting into words, though I so desperately want to. And there's only one person in my life who I can even begin to articulate this confusing pain to, but I don't want to place all my burden on Nick alone. So, that leaves me feeling disconnected from the world around me, in my own sunken place and that much more lost.

Gucci was most likely referring to being lost in success and letting your clout or your accomplishments get the best of you. But I believe we can also find ourselves lost in our hardships. All of this—the confusion, the missing map, the school work, the sappy love story, the loneliness—just might also be the "sauce" that Gucci was talking about too. These are all the hurdles of life that a man could find himself lost without (because these are necessary hurdles for our growth).

Nevertheless, a man with too much can find himself lost within these types of hurdles as well. In this context, I view the "sauce" as both our adversity and our successes. Just because someone may seem saucy (or highly successful) doesn't mean they are happy or not without guidance. Take me, for example. I double majored at one of the best schools in the nation; I've traveled across the world (okay mostly across the US, but nearly all for free); I'm creating my own startup; and I've built a global network (yes, my LinkedIn is flames), although, I still feel lost. There seems to be a slight layer of depression blanketing my soul.

This has taught me that success, even your hardest earned accomplishments, can't help you find yourself. That discovery has to come from within. So as Mr. Davis would probably say, be wary of the sauce.

LOST IN THE SAUCE

Being "lost" can mean more than just feeling depressed or anxious. It's possible to also feel lost about who you are, or who you want to be. Just like how I've fallen victim to my hardships, I've also fallen victim to my identity as well. What I mean is that I've gotten "lost in the sauce" in not knowing what kind of person I want to become or which of my passions I want to follow.

Toward the beginning of my junior year of college, I began to question the career path I wanted to pursue after graduation. I had just finished my internship at Bloomberg LP and was already on the hunt for next summer's opportunity. I was searching for another marketing internship because that's what I was devoted to.

For as long as I can remember, I have always had a love for business. My childhood best friend use to tell me, "Jerome, you could sell the shirt off someone's back!" I would laugh it off because I never thought I deserved that much credit.

Mark was one of my first true friends, and he always gave the best compliments, but maybe he was onto something. Even though I didn't like embracing it, that's really who I was... who I am—a go-getter by nature.

I was constantly finding new ways to make a dollar and establish my independence when I was growing up, whether I was mowing lawns, washing cars, cleaning gutters, burning and selling CDs, or moving so much candy in middle school that I barely had enough space in my backpack for books. Yet, even when my operation had grown so much that I had other students selling the candy for me, and Ziploc bagged exchanges of skittles for cash was all I had to do, I still didn't think of myself as a "businessman."

It wasn't until the end of seventh grade when I signed up for a summer Biz-Camp that I finally felt verified as a young businessman. The camp was hosted by a nonprofit called Youth Entrepreneurship South Carolina or YESCarolina. They taught me how to properly run a company and they empowered me with the skills to be an entrepreneur. That program ended up changing my life forever.

In eighth grade, YESCarolina named me as the Youth Entrepreneur of the Year for South Carolina! To this day, I can't believe the connections I've made and lessons I was able to learn all because I decided to do a three-week summer camp and start a handyman service. I called the company The HandyKid.

I share that story because it shows how deeply rooted my passion for business actually is. That's the reason why I came to Georgetown to major in marketing. But as you know from my introduction and the first chapter, I was exposed to a whole new world of knowledge when I got to college. Those views, ideas, and truths reshaped how I viewed the world around me. It reshaped how I viewed myself. And if I can be honest with you, it left me feeling a little lost too.

Between my liberal arts courses and engaging with different activist on campus, I discovered so much about the vast injustices that marginalized communities face. While I was learning all these things, I also found out how I wanted to give back to my community. I've tutored at-risk youth in DC, taught fifth graders entrepreneurship, created a safe space for men of color on campus, and started my own mentorship organization (I obviously had a calling for youth development). I was shown the problems that faced my younger brothers and sisters, and my immediate response was to help.

But all of this left me questioning if a career in corporate America was still something I wanted. I began to feel like America's capitalism was the direct source of a lot of the problems I saw my community struggling with.

Can you imagine how hard it is to suddenly feel so conflicted about what you always dreamed of doing since you were young?

I felt guilty for wanting to get a corporate job. I felt like I left Charleston for profit. I felt like my people needed me to be something more. I felt like my passion for business was directly at odds with my passion for youth development. I felt lost.

What got me through this internal conflict was taking the time to reevaluate myself and what my best interests were. Self-awareness is the most powerful tool you can possess as a person. If you know yourself—your skills, your weakness, your fears, your short-fallings, your joys, your insecurities, etc.—you can always find your way out of a dark and lost situation. And that's exactly what I did.

After reflecting, I reminded myself that I made it this far by following what I loved and working toward my passions. There was no point in stopping that now. Even though my interests may have shifted, I knew I had to continue to give these new ideas the same level of attention and energy. If I wanted happiness, I needed to let my passion lead my life. The money and the resources will eventually come. But happiness is never guaranteed.

Realizing this and embracing this mentality was how I got myself out of feeling so lost (for a second time). Then, I practiced what I preached and started giving my all to the things I was passionate about. I expanded the outreach of my mentorship organization. I collaborated with a nonprofit to start a new Saturday School program at a local middle school. And let's not forget, I started writing this book!

Doing what I love has helped me feel comfortable in knowing that I can always find a way to be myself, no matter where I am. I will admit, I am still not sure where I'm going next, but I do know that I don't feel lost about how I'm going to get there.

POWER OF POSITIVITY

The best way to fight hate is with love. And the best way to balance the negatives is with positivity. Even in my lowest moments, I still found ways to make myself smile by appreciating the silver lining of every situation. Depression's best friend is pessimism. If you can't find joy in the situation you're in, you're bound to spiral. I use my love for myself, my love for what I do, and my excitement for what my future holds as a way to get me through my toughest times.

When I leave an exam and I know I failed it, I don't dwell on the past. I think about how I can do better on the next one. And if there isn't going to be a next one, I accept that what's done is done. The universe has spoken, and there's nothing I can do about it. A part of my positivity comes from knowing that I can only control the controllable. Everything else is out of my hands.

But positive thinking was something I harnessed way before I was failing college exams. I told you about my mom in chapter 3, and how I struggled with her being in and out of prison my entire life. I could have easily used my upbringing as an excuse to be mad at the world. Instead, I used it as a means of motivation.

If you remember, I called myself her soldier because I felt like I had to always fight for her to stay home. Every time the state would take her away from me, I felt more and more driven to do better in school. I thought that if I made straight As I could make her proud enough to want to stay home and stop committing those crimes. Whenever she caught a new charge, I was motivated all over again. I doubt I would have worked that hard if my life was easier. That's the power of positivity.

Keeping a positive outlook also got some of my friends through really tough times as well. I told you about the story of how my friend Jordan got arrested my freshman year in chapter 1. (It's crazy to think about how much mass incarceration has played a significant role in my life.) He served a little over a year in jail. From what he told me, that was the lowest point of his entire life. And even though I knew nothing but pain and stress was weighing on his soul, he always had a positive attitude whenever we got on the phone. Those fifteen minute were never long enough, but they were always filled with laughs and outrageous plans for when he got out.

If we weren't cracking jokes or going down memory lane, he was telling me all about the new book he had just read that week or some new insight he wanted to share with me.

"I hate being here, but I feel like this was what I needed to get my life together," he told me one day over the phone.

When he said this, I felt my tear ducts begin to swell. But these weren't just melancholy tears that were forming. They were tears of both joy and sadness because even though my childhood friend since fourth grade had lost his freedom, I got to witness him liberate himself at the same time. That's the power of positivity.

There are countless stories I could share about how an optimistic view can change everything. You don't have to be going through a life-changing situation to need positivity in your life, though. Cultivating a more positive outlook on the world takes consistency more than anything else. In fact, you're less likely to be able to keep yourself in high spirits during your most difficult times if you've never practiced it.

The simple things have the power to brighten our day the most. Take time to figure out what those things are for you. We live in a negative world, and it can be easy to find yourself lost in that negativity. Sometimes it seems like we have to hunt for our happiness, but it's up to us to be our own best pep-talker and to remind ourselves what we're grateful for. If you can learn to do this, you can learn to tap into one of the most important ingredients needed to overcome being lost in the sauce—hope.

TAKEAWAYS

Takeaway #1

For this chapter, your greatest takeaway is to find your "why." What motivates you to get you through work or class or practice? I treat my "why" like gasoline to my engine. If I ever lose place of it, I know I won't be running for too much longer. I told you at the beginning of the chapter that I felt like my internal roadmap was missing, and without it I was lost. It wasn't until I reminded myself of my convictions that I found my way again. Being aware of why it is you do what you do can work wonders in your life. When I knew what I was working toward, I tended to have a little more pep in my step.

I envision our passions, what drives us, as a metaphorical rope that we all need when we feel ourselves sinking deeper and deeper into the "sauce." When we find our "why," we find our rope that we use to pull ourselves out of the slumps of depression. You have to be sure not to let yourself idle in lostness for too long because the longer you're there, the harder it becomes to pull yourself out. Allison Hilton once told me, "Young people who are lost turn into adults who are lost."

We can't afford to have any more lost adults.

Takeaway #2

My next takeaway for you is all about self-care. I think self-care gets highly overlooked when we're young. But in all actuality, it is something everyone should practice. By definition, self-care is any form of care done by one's self that doesn't require medical or professional consultation. Self-care can, technically, refer to any kind healthcare treatment done by oneself for the betterment of one's health and wellness. But the kind of self-care I'm talking about is one of self-enrichment for the mind and soul.

I'm talking about self-care for your mental health. For me, I'm always finding ways to practice self-care day in and day out. It's the only way I stay above water amidst all the pressures I face. One of the biggest saviors of my sanity has been my best friend. He doesn't know this, but our daily check-ins have become one of my fundamental self-care practices. But not only do I use him as a sounding board, I also find it refreshing every time I get to share my story with other students who have had similar experiences.

I feed my body with good food, exercise, and naps, naps, naps, and more naps (a college student's best friend). Then I feed my spirit and soul with good music, my favorite TV shows, meditation, prayer, and reflection. I also practice self-care by reminding myself what I'm thankful for and by journaling as often as I can.

Now, I don't practice all of these things every day, but I do tailor my regimen to meet my emotional needs at any given time. Self-care is how I keep myself in high spirits and balanced. Have you figured out your own system of self-care yet?

Takeaway #3

My last takeaway comes from one of my mentors back home. I met with him one day just to catch up, and in doing so, I opened up to him about the rut I found myself in the semester before (the same rut from my opening story). As soon as I was done talking, I could see that he instantly felt my pain. He was saddened to see that I had fallen into a depression.

"Jerome, I'm so sorry to hear that," he empathized with me. "Listen, I'm going to share with you my five personal tips I follow every day to maintain my energy and happiness. You ready?" I nodded. "Then write this down…"

1. **Constantly learn and grow**: Expanding your mind has a funny way of expanding your heart at the same time. As you learn new things about the world, you also discover new things about yourself. And self-love and inner happiness are

directly contingent upon self-awareness. I'm a firm believer that you cannot love (or truly be happy with) what you don't know. Plus, learning new things is always fascinating!

2. **Goal attainment is key:** You have to count your wins—no matter how small—every step of the way. If all you do is dwell on your losses, it's only a matter of time before you start seeing yourself as a loser. Be proud of your accomplishments! That pride will keep you moving forward.

3. **Be optimistic:** He and I couldn't agree more on this one. Similar to tip number 2, don't get bogged down in the negatives. If you don't allow yourself to see the possibilities, there will never be any. You have to be excited about what's to come! Without that excitement, what do you have making you want to wake up in the morning?

4. **Maintain control over your destiny:** This tip is directly correlated with pimping the system. You have to believe that your actions matter, and whether you succeed or fail is based on the decisions *you* made. You can't allow yourself to feel as though no matter how hard you work,

your outcomes will never change. That's the definition of despair—hopelessness. Control your destiny, control your happiness.

5. **Foster quality relationships**: Quality relationships aren't just good for when you need someone to depend on. They are also a great source of constant joy. Having people you can laugh with is just as necessary as having people you can cry with, and vice versa. We crave human connection and love. Quality relationships satisfy those needs for us and make us feel whole.

CHAPTER 5

THE MASSES ARE ASSES

___

TRUE STORY #5

Some names and identifying details have been changed to protect the privacy and safety of individuals. Meanwhile, other identifying details may have been dramatized for the purpose of enhancing the story.

"Jerome ain't never been in an accident *and* he got straight As, Granny! I promise you he won't do nothing stupid with your car!" Is what my best friend, Mel, said as he vouched for my character.

"Yeah Mel ain't lying either! Plus, this is basically a real license. Look. See?" I said as I handed his grandma my ID with the utmost confidence.

We were all no older than fifteen years old, and I had recently gotten my restricted license and could finally drive on my own. Technically, I wasn't supposed to be on the roads at night without someone at least twenty-one years old in the car, but we made sure to keep that requisite out of our negotiation tactic.

We showed Mel's grandma my brand new driver's license and begged to borrow her truck for the evening. She knew I was the most responsible one out of the group and she trusted me. After twenty minutes of nagging, she finally tossed us the keys to her fiery red, two-door '98 Ford Explorer. The middle console was missing, the gas meter was a "floater," and the black paint on the buttons of the radio had rubbed off so much that they were all indistinguishable, but to us that Explorer might as well have been a Bentley! We were sophomores in high school and we had a car on a Saturday night. It was about—to go—down!

"Ha-ha! I can't believe she said yeah," I told Mel. "Call up Keenan and let him know we 'bout to scoop him up and head over to Mimi's house party tonight."

Mel and I went to pick up Keenan and somehow ended up with Chase, CJ, Mike and Big Lip Taz joining us. Word spread fast that we had a car for the evening, but those four live right around the corner from the party, so it wasn't too much hassle. The truck was packed: two up front, three in the backseat, and two in the cargo area. Having two people ride in the trunk of the SUV would be the first of many laws we ended up breaking that night. (Well, I guess the second, I was already driving at night pass my license's curfew.)

We pulled up to the party blasting "LIL BIG DAWGIN" by VT as loud as the Explorer's stock speakers would let us. Parking on Mimi's narrow road was scarce so I decided to parallel park right across the street in front of her house. The red truck and loud music drew everyone's attention.

But you couldn't tell us nothing!

"Man hurry up, Rome, so you can let us out!" shouted Chase from the trunk.

Everyone in the car was ready to dance with a few girls and walk away with a few phone numbers too by the end of the night. We cracked the usual jokes about how Keenan wasn't going to do either and then stepped out of the car. As we approached the house I remember getting a weird vibe. The music wasn't particularly loud. There was just something "off" about the whole thing. Chase and Big Lip Taz were up front, followed by CJ, Mike, Mel, Keenan, and me as anchor.

There was a group of guys on either side of the front door, like a team of bouncers for a club. They were wearing all black. Most of them had on hoodies with their hoodlaces tied tightly underneath their chin. The way their hoodies were tied up only left a small circle with just enough space to show their eyes, nose, and mouth, but I recognized them instantly. They were no friends of ours. In fact, one could say they were enemies. These boys were part of a local gang in Charleston that was causing a lot of noise in the city. And usually, you don't have to worry about gang violence if you don't have beef with anyone yourself; they typically don't cause trouble for no reason.

But that wasn't the case for us.

None of us were officially banging by any means. That wasn't a life any of us chose to live. However, because of who Chase and Keenan's older brothers were, whether or not we banged became irrelevant. And just that quick, our friends' beef became our beef due to technicality. Tension immediately filled the party. We were seen as the opposition. We were just the right little fishes they needed to catch the bigger fishes they couldn't get ahold of. Essentially, we were the enemy. We were a target. And we were greatly outnumbered.

My heart sank when I heard TJ whisper, "Oh that's the nigga that wanna fight Lil' Smoke." A crowd of affirming voices followed him.

I knew he was talking about me because I had heard that same rumor earlier in school that week, but I had no idea it had spread that quickly. I didn't want to fight anybody. I didn't even know where that came from. My hands started to tremble a little, but all my homies seemed unfazed. So I clenched my fists, gave them a cold side eye and kept it pushing. I couldn't afford to let them know how scared I was.

We entered the party, but the joy we just had five minutes ago in the car had been sucked out of us. For the most part, everyone was aware of the situation we just walked into. I knew Chase was in the greatest danger because of his brother's role in the opposing gang. But I couldn't find him anywhere.

"Yo, you seen Chase?" I asked Mel nervously.

"Yeah, Mike said him and Taz walked out the back door and hopped the fence. They already know what time it is."

"Bro we need to slide too."

"I know."

We needed an escape plan and we didn't have one. The tension only grew in the house as time went on. Nobody was dancing; they were all just standing around. It was like everyone was aware of what was about to happen. I just knew we were going to get jumped, or worse. Every minute seemed like an hour. I felt myself getting more and more paranoid. Mel and Keenan appeared so calm but I could see the worry in their eyes too.

The situation got real when one of them came up to Mel and started talking to him. Rashard never had any beef with Mel. They knew each other because of football, and there was a level of mutual respect between the two of them. His relationship with Keenan, on the other hand, was a different story. I didn't know much about Rashard, but I knew he had just gotten out of jail, and Keenan had been talking to his girlfriend while he was away.

"Bruh, what he say to you?" I asked Mel as Rashard walked back over to join the other wannabe bouncers.

"He asked me if Keenan was Kelley's little brother," Mel responded, finally, with the same level of concern I had felt all along. Rashard knew that Keenan and Kelley were brothers already—everyone knew that already. He was trying to intimidate us. I guess as a way of payback for all the times Kelley must've intimidated him.

"It's time for us to GO, bruh"

"No duh, Rome," Mel snapped back.

"Then let's slide, nigga!"

"How, Rome? How? You think they gonna let us just walk out the front door, bruh?"

He was right. There was no way in hell it was going to go down like that. Then out of nowhere God blessed us with our window of opportunity. We could hear some commotion going on in the street. The music had subsided by this point, and all you could hear was chatter amongst the crowd. There was a weird buzz of voices vibrating throughout the party. The bouncers, all of them, left their posts on the porch to investigate what all the fuss was about down the street. I looked Mel and Keenan in the eyes and it was almost telepathic how quickly we got each other's message.

Since Mike and CJ didn't have anything to worry about in the party (the focus was on Chase, Keenan, and me), we told them to walk to the stop sign at the corner and wait for us there. It would've taken too long to have them climb into the truck since it was a two-door model. Meanwhile, me, Keenan, and Mel moved swiftly toward the exit. I stood in the middle of the door frame like a nosey neighbor and I saw for myself what the confusion was. Off into the distance, I could see a group of dudes walking down the middle of the street. It was a gang of them.

"That's dem boys from off the Rum!" I heard one of the bouncers yell in the Geechiest of tones.

It was like something out of a ghetto Western standoff. The boys from Romney Street and all the dudes from the party were standing in the middle of the road. Half to the left of me, half to the right. And our car was dead smack in the middle of them across the street. I looked at Keenan and Mel, and again, with no words I asked them, "Do you see this shit?"

We jogged through the foggy street and heated exchange of words. I fumbled with the keys as I tried to recover my nerves.

"Hurry the fuck up, Rome!" I don't even remember which one of them said that.

Finally, we got in the truck and proceeded to pull off. The damn street was so narrow, there was no way I was going to successfully make a U-turn. My driver's ed training had to kick in. So there I was, performing the most awkward three-point turn in the history of mankind, under the most stressful of situations. I could feel Keenan and Mel burning a hole into the side of my face with their eyes of anxiety and frustration.

The car fishtailed in the gravel as we made it in the clear. I pulled over at the stop sign to see that Mike and CJ had followed directions. They hopped inside the whip yelling, "Go! Go! Go! Go! Go! Go! Go!" And that's exactly what I did, skirting off before the doors were even closed.

"Where Taz and Chase at?" I asked

"I don't know. Somebody call them," Keenan demanded.

"They by the church 'round the corner," answered CJ.

It didn't take us long to find them. Taz walked up to the door expecting to get the same spot in the back seat he had before. He was fussing and what not.

"Bruh, if you don't get yo big, goofy ass in the gotdamn trunk, I'ma leave you and yo big ass lip." I was so pissed off. He was acting like a child.

That area near the party was getting too much attention. We needed somewhere to lay low and regather ourselves. We decided to go to Chase's Granny's house because it wasn't too far from where we were. I pulled into the driveway recklessly. All seven of us evacuated the Explorer, furious.

"Man, screw dem niggas, dawg! Word! I swear to God dey gone pay." Chase was the most furious of us all.

It wasn't long before it came time to make some phone calls. Chase called his brother and CJ called Kelley on Keenan's behalf. For me, Mel, and Keenan, this wasn't our first rodeo. We were just glad we could call the night an overall success (nobody was hurt). But everyone else insisted that measures needed to be taken. Kelley and his friends must've already been on their way because in less than ten minutes, we heard doors slamming and hollering outside. They had pulled up in a small, black, rental car. They were heavily armed and even madder than us.

"Y'all boy straight? Everything good? They ain't touch y'all init?"

"Nahh, we straight they ain't do shit," we all responded.

"Where them niggas at, bubba?" The question was directed toward Chase.

He and his brother walked away from the rest of us as Chase gave him a recount of what had just happened. And just as fast as they arrived, they were gone. We all stood outside in the driveway trying to make sense of it all.

I was puzzled. "Y'all think they going wet that shit up?" I asked.

No one responded. I guess my question was rhetorical. We stood there for about five minutes without saying much until our silence was broken by the distant ring of gun shots. And lots of it. I felt like I was listening to someone play Call of Duty in the background. My question was answered… I was fearful of what the outcome of the rest of the night would be.

I couldn't help but think that what just happened was our fault. I don't think I could have lived with myself if anyone got hurt, which thankfully no one was injured (thank God for their lack of aim). I can remember thinking, *This isn't who I am. This isn't what I should be getting myself involved with. This isn't me.*

But I didn't have time to dwell on that. I could hear the police sirens closing in, and the last thing I needed was to get stuck on this side of town due to the inevitable road blocks and heightened patrol I knew was bound to follow. Mike, CJ and Big Lip Taz all agreed to stay at Chase's grandma's house for the night. That just left the rest of us to get to Dorchester road.

I was ready for us to go back to my house and put this night behind us. Police cars headed to the crime scene rushed past me as we left Chase's house. I could feel my heart racing. The music was playing low, but my chest was vibrating as if the bass in the speakers were turned all the way up. I could barely focus on the road. We were halfway to the house when Keenan's phone rang. It was Kelley.

"What's up?" Keenan answered. There was a long pause. I remember because I was listening intently. "Alright, alright. Where you at?" Another pause. "Okay, I'll tell Rome."

"'Tell Rome' what?" I questioned as soon as the call ended.

"Kelley say he stuck on the Four and him and his homeboy ain't got no ride," Keenan answered. "He need you to come scoop them. They hot right now."

This night just kept getting longer. I thought I would never make it home. We approached a red light and I leaned my head back onto the seat as I gave a long and tired exhale. I couldn't consider myself a true homeboy if I wasn't down to ride for him when he needed me most. That's exactly what he just did for me. I looked at Mel and asked for his approval, "You cool with us using your granny truck to get them?" Mel nodded his head.

So much for not doing anything stupid with the car tonight.

———

It didn't take us long to get to them. There was a porch full of dudes wearing all black when we arrived to this mysterious house in the hood. They almost looked like the wannabe bouncers we just left at Mimi's house, but I knew these boys weren't "wannabe" anything. Four of them stepped off the porch. One of them was Kelley. He walked up to the passenger window and asked me to unlock the trunk so his two other homeboys could get in.

"I thought you said it was only two of y'all?" I could feel the frustration building inside me. This, *all of this,* was not what I signed up for.

"They need a ride too, bruh. We all going to the same place, bruh, don't act like that." Kelley always knew how to give just the right amount of information beforehand to get me to agree to something.

"Alright, man. Come on."

They all piled into the extremely noticeable and characteristically loud red truck. I looked in the rearview mirror to see one of the biggest revolvers I'd ever seen in my life (I think it was a Smith & Wesson 500 Magnum) in the hands of a man I've never met before. He held up the gun to check his ammo, as if his mission was not complete for the evening. The light from the street lamp came through the back window just enough for me to get a glimpse of the massive barrel. Was I bout to go to jail for some men I didn't even know?

Kelley followed my wary eyes in the rearview mirror and knew exactly what was troubling me.

"Yeah, we got some big boy guns in here, bubba," he confirmed, "But, just act normal and drive carefully and we'll all be straight."

"Yeah, bruh. And if ball pull us over we gone hop out and run. Just say we forced y'all to drive us," added one of his unknown accessories.

Their plan would never work that easily. The Explorer only had two doors, but I appreciated them trying to put my mind at ease. I could feel moisture building under my palms as I gripped the steering wheel. Ten and two. The car was silent. No words. No radio. I could barely hear anyone breathe. (I guess we were all holding our breath.) The sound of a loud

V8 engine that needed an oil change was all I had to soothe me. It was only a three-mile drive to get to Collins Park, but this was also the worst time of night to be in a car full of Black teenagers on Dorchester road with North Charleston Police officers lurking.

I couldn't believe what I had gotten myself into that night. "How in the world did we get to this point?" I asked myself. As I struggled to remember everything I'd ever learned in driver's ed, Kendrick Lamar's, "The Art of Peer Pressure" slipped into my mind. Halfway to Collins Park, the two guys in the trunk interrupted my concentration with jokes about how fast those dudes back at Mimi's party started running when they began shooting. I chuckled. In my head, I felt like those punks deserved it, but in my heart I knew it was wrong.

This made me think about Kendrick's line in the song when he said, "I never was a gangbanger. I mean, I never was a stranger to the fonk neither. I really doubt it. Rush a nigga quick then we laugh about it. That's ironic, 'cause I've never been violent, until I'm with the homies."

With the radio off, that song kept replaying in my head. I never smoked weed. I never had a gun in the car. I never thought about retaliating against people. I never screamed, "fuck the police." I never thought about my life ending.

Until I was with the homies...

We finally made it to where we were going and dropped off Kelley and his friends. Afterward, Keenan, Mel, and I went back to my house where we could finally call it a night. We told Mel's grandma that we'd return the car in the morning. As I took off my shoes and sat on the edge of my bed, I still had K-Dot's "The Art of Peer Pressure" playing in my head. There was one line in particular that I echoed throughout my mind, "One lucky night with the homies."

THE MASSES ARE ASSES

I read an article once that said Gen Z (anyone born from 1996 to 2012) values individuality and creativity more than any other generation to date. I found that very interesting. The article went on to say that Gen Zers embrace uniqueness while also defying social norms. As everyone in this generation strives to be different, they rely on their creativity to find new and artistic ways to express themselves. This generation is seen as trailblazers who are ready to create social change. All their lives, they've been told they were special and that the world is theirs for the taking. And, according to this article, that's what they've come to believe.

I was born on November 11, 1996. That puts me right at the cusp between being a Millennial and Gen Z. Even though it feels a little bit like I'm in limbo between the two, I mostly identify as Gen Z. I consider myself as part of the "digital natives" who are fighting for social good. Not to brag, but I also like to believe that I possess the creativity and wittiness that comes with being a member of Gen Z. And for a long time, I really thought of myself as a true individual—in every sense of the word.

I used to tell myself in high school, "There's no other seventeen-year-old in the state of South Carolina working as hard as you."

Whether this was accurate or not wasn't the point. The point was that I believed what I was doing was special and personal. I saw my roles as a motivational speaker, my school's ambassador, an honor roll student, and the president of my DECA chapter as all being a part of my identity.

Not only did I navigate those spaces fluently, I also never lost my street credibility in the process. I could code-switch effortlessly between the hood dudes who stood in the back of the cafeteria and my Drama Studio classmates who lived in Shadow Moss. In both of these cases, I always felt like I was in my element.

I saw it as two parts of my identity. As if it were two languages I had come to understand and speak. At no point did I ever think I wasn't being my authentic self. Regardless if I was with my bros smoking weed and playing 2K, or with my AP classmates listening to Ed Sheeran as we worked on a group assignment, I still felt like I was expressing my individuality.

But then I think about stories like the one I just told you (there are plenty more where that came from). Where was my individuality then? My seventeen-year-old self would claim that he had so much emotional intelligence and a mind of his own, but still would allow himself and the boys he loved to be placed in harm's way.

I knew exactly what type of party I was driving us to that night. I also knew there was a high chance that the boys from the other side were going to be there. (I just didn't anticipate so many of them.) And I knew what the result would be if we told Kelley and his homeboys, yet we called them anyway.

If I really believed in expressing myself, I would have expressed to my friends that we shouldn't have been involving ourselves in all those things we took part in. Looking back on that time of my life, I realized I wasn't that much of an

individual at all when I was around my friends. I /
"Jerome the Motivational Speaker" or "The Voice of West
Ashley" anymore when I was with them. Instead, I became
just like every other Geechee delinquent from Charleston;
the ones who were overly concerned about finding some
"pressure" (high grade weed) and packing a "scrap" (a gun)
at every function.

In hindsight, maybe that's why a part of me enjoyed that
reckless lifestyle so much. Maybe I just wanted to prove that
I was still just like them, that I was normal. But to be normal
means to be average. And their ain't shit "unique" about
being average. This double lifestyle I chose to live was just
nonsense, but I didn't see it for what it was until I turned
eighteen.

We were supposed to be the generation of individuals
who roamed without labels. We were supposed to be the
creative youth who used our talents to spark change within
our community. At least, that's what the article said. But in
actuality, what I saw back home was a group of peers who
were all trying to be like one another.

All the kids dressed the same, acted the same, talked the
same, and inevitably, thought the same. Now, I'm not saying
sharing characteristics with those around you is a bad thing.

That definition makes culture and community. But such a like mindedness does become a problem when the mindset everyone has come to share is a destructive one.

———

This is usually the part where I include another story from one of the people I interviewed for this book, but I think my story says it all. You may not have ever abused a substance or gotten tangled up in gang violence (which is good, I hope you never do), but you probably can relate to doing things that were out of your character in an attempt to fit in. The art of peer pressure is a mighty force, and I've seen it eat kids whole. There were plenty of times when I should have been arrested. And there were a few more times when I could have been killed. This left me to wonder, *Were my friendships worth any of this?*

Not to be mistaken, I love all of those boys. I really do. (Except for Kelley's two friends in the trunk; I didn't know who the hell they were.) My love runs deep for all my day-one friends—Mel, Keenan, Kelley, Vernon, Jordan, and Henry. Most of us share memories that go as far back as third grade. I love those boys so much that, even to this day, I'm willing to put my life on the line for them. I'd take a bullet for any one of those guys if it was necessary.

However, that night was not necessary. It was far from it. It was nonsense. It was stupid. It was reckless. Innocent lives could have been lost in vain. And at what cost? Over some beef that neither side could even pinpoint the origins of? Because some young high schoolers felt threatened? This wasn't the type of ideology I ever believed in, but it was the ideology I seemed to continuously condone. My conviction was spineless.

I considered myself a motivational speaker. I was the Youth Entrepreneur of the Year for South Carolina. My mayor proclaimed July 28 as Jerome Smalls Day in Charleston County. I had Senator Tim Scott's personal phone number on speed dial. I was a part of the school's drama studio. I did the morning announcements and was on a first name basis with my principal for crying out loud. Yet—there I was, so easily persuaded by the pressures of my peers. I say all of this to tell you that peer pressure, and getting caught at the wrong place at the wrong time, can happen to anyone.

Looking back on it, my peers, as individuals, weren't the sole root of the problem. We are all products of our environment. Our communities shaped us the most. What we saw was all we knew, and that's no fault of our own. The notion of, "That's what everyone else is doing" was always in the backs of our minds.

Sure, we were fearful in moments like the one I shared. Who wouldn't be? But that fear never carried over into the next day. And it sure didn't stop us from getting Mel's grandmother's truck again the following weekend and going to yet another party. Of course we were more cautious, more aware, but just as foolish. Because that's just how things were. Sometimes you got into trouble. Sometimes you didn't.

People would constantly ask me why I surrounded myself with friends who, from the surface, seemed like such bad influences. My response was always simple. Sure, they may have been a bad influence on me in certain ways, but my true friends—the ones I can still call on today—have always been good, loving people at heart. And we were just some knuckleheaded teens trying to find our way through life.

Given that I was the product of the same environment, one could argue I even peer pressured them many times. Nevertheless, I like to believe that my positive influence on them was far greater than their negative influence on me. And if that net positive outcome resulted in one of their lives being saved, all of that risk was worth it.

Granted, it took me being removed from it all and coming to college to see just how risky those weekends and summer nights really were. Often times I thought of my name in the headlines of the local news for all the wrong reasons, "Youth Entrepreneur Shot & Killed at North Charleston Party." I also thought about how quickly I could've ruined the reputation I had built for myself. Or how I could've lost every shot I had at ever getting into Georgetown.

We thought of ourselves as men, but in reality we were boys. Our actions were childish. We were just kids. After a few years of review, I realized we weren't lacking proper parenting (we had great parents), nor were we lacking guidance (we knew what we were supposed to be doing), however, what we lacked was identity. Our poor choices came about as a result of our weak self-knowledge.

It wasn't until I learned who I truly was that I was able to know in my heart what I valued. When you discover what you dislike, saying no becomes a lot easier. As a teenager, I thought I liked going to those parties that only ended with gun shots or police intervention because that's what my homies enjoyed (and they probably shared the same mentality as me—which means we were all just part of this puzzled cycle). I found pleasure degrading women behind closed doors because that garnered the most laughs and respect amongst my boys.

I thought everyone liked getting high all the time and singing along to their favorite songs because that's all I saw on Snapchat. But none of that was ever *my* interests. I enjoyed taking girls out on dates like in the movies, only smoking on special occasions, making music with my crew, and cracking jokes with my friends as we chilled and enjoyed each other's company.

What happened that night was not a rare incident for us. We got lucky time and time again. During each one of those times I found myself taking turns down pathways I never would have gone down on my own. Granted, I stuck by my guns enough to balance my good decisions with my poor decisions and I managed to come out on top. However, I have friends who either weren't as good at balancing, or weren't as lucky as I was.

Even though we all had distinctive personalities and different views on the world, we were also all one in the same. We allowed ourselves to influence each other in ways that we still have yet to fully understand. They say you are your five closest friends. For me, my five closest friends (really six) spent so much time together that, as a unit, we were one. We shared mannerisms, lingo, clothes, girls, music, you name it. But we also shared a level of ignorance that almost got us killed on multiple occasions.

Understanding the different types of energy we fed off from one another has taught me a valuable lesson. I learned that following the ways of everyone else (AKA the masses) can leave you looking like a moron (AKA an ass). Without knowing yourself, you lack a sense of direction, allowing others to direct your path for you. If you find that your identity isn't rooted in something, it's only a matter of time before the wind takes you where it pleases.

TAKEAWAY

The lesson here is simple: Take the time to learn who you are, and then stay true to that person. Be yourself by any means necessary. Your life may depend on it.

CHAPTER 6

OWNERSHIP

TRUE STORY #6

I was nineteen when someone told me that the prison industrial complex used the failure rates of third graders to determine how many jail cells they'll need to account for in the future. When I first heard this, it was like a frozen snake ran down my spine. I immediately thought back on my own poor performance as a third grader. When I could barely read and my ability to trace my name came solely from muscle memory and not because I actually knew how to spell it (especially my middle name... that tripped me up the most). But what made my spine especially cold was when I paired this chilling news with the vivid image of the brand new jail that was just completed, at the time, back in my hometown. I was eighteen when the Sheriff Al Cannon Detention Center opened for business.

I couldn't help but think, "Damn, they were expecting me to be there."

One of the hardest truths I had to learn was how difficult it is for Black and low-income students to succeed within America's educational system. It felt like we were never meant to thrive here. Thankfully, I discovered that the correlation between illiterate third graders and future convicts wasn't true, at least not completely. However, that fact check didn't rid me of my chills. The school-to-prison pipeline is still a reality for many kids across the country, my friends included.

Wanna know a statistic that is true? One in three of all African-American men can expect themselves to end up in jail at least once in their life. Wanna know something even crazier? Out of my six childhood best friends (me included), two of them have been arrested. Basic math will tell you that two in six simplifies to what? One in three.

Just like my mom, I know my friends made their own beds. They broke the law and had to pay the price. Regardless of their mistakes, this was just one of the many statistics that were (and still are) heavily stacked against us. Numbers like these can suck the morale out of any student, and make you want to give up. I know many times it almost did for me. Since my struggle with the English language in third grade, I've always known I was going to have to push myself in school. Remember what I said in the introduction about having to stay two steps ahead of everyone else so they never learned I actually started three steps behind? Well, that's exactly the type of fight I've had to put up all throughout elementary school, middle school, high school, and even college.

I've gotten used to these battles, but they haven't become any less tiring. Don't get me wrong, I love these moments of combat, though—when I'm forced to reread, question myself, or Google things in secrecy—because I learn best in those moments. One of the most important things I've learned, as I continue to enter the ring time and time again, is that no one else is going to fight this war for me. In other words, I would be a fool to think I could depend on someone else for my success. No one is going to fill out *my* applications, complete *my* assignments, or take *my* tests because they have their own battles to fight. That ownership falls on me, and the same applies to you.

Taking ownership over your education can be one of the hardest things to do as a kid, especially if you're not good at it. Thankfully, I had grandparents who sat me down at the coffee table every day after school to do my homework. Papa would put math in terms of money and Nana would quiz me on my vocabulary with flashcards. But as you get older and school gets harder, your parents and guardians become less and less of a resource. Papa didn't know how to use nickels and quarters anymore to help me solve for X when I was taking algebra, but that didn't stop him from still checking in on me either.

By the time I reached high school, I was pretty much an honor roll student. I had that "spark" that made me want to learn. I'm sure my friends would just say I was a nerd (which is probably true). Eventually, good grades were just something my grandparents came to expect. Those check-ins became less frequent and it got to the point where I didn't have anyone looking over my shoulder to make sure I was staying afloat anymore. Which I guess isn't a bad thing, but it did make me feel as though the only support group I had, academically, was myself.

The onus was on me, but I grew comfortable with this type of ownership. None of my friends were in the same classes as me, and I became blind to the fact that I was always one of two or three Black students in my AP courses. No to mention, my Nana had no idea what type of homework I was doing, but I was fine with all of that because I knew all of this work was going toward me getting into college. Much like the A's on my report card every quarter, me getting a degree somewhere was just another one of those things everyone expected, "Of course Jerome's going to college."

Yet, all the academic responsibility in the world couldn't have prepared me for when that time actually came. The summer going into my senior year of high school was full of rude awakenings. I quickly learned that talking about college and being about college were two totally different things.

Since ninth grade, I knew that West Ashley High School was not going to be the climax of my educational career. For some of my friends it was, and that's perfectly fine, I just never considered it as part of my plan. But even though I always felt destined to go to college, the summer of 2014 showed me that I had no idea where I wanted to go or how I was going to get there.

It wasn't like I was a top, perspective athlete who had schools all over the country asking me to choose them. (I sucked at football.) I needed a way to stand out so they would choose me. I was just another student, with a slightly above average SAT score, praying that my personal statement could make dreams come true.

I began to worry toward the end of junior year. I was absolutely clueless about the college application process, but I couldn't let everyone else know that. So I asked certain questions to certain people and I absorbed information from *everyone.*

I realized I wasn't as privileged as a lot of my peers. I didn't have parents or grandparents or cousins or many friends who went to college. I didn't have anyone in my immediate circle who I could talk to about how to choose the right school, what FAFSA was, what "100% Need-Blind" meant, the benefits of going to a big school versus a small school, what I could expect dorm life to be like, and the list goes on. At least when it came to me being on my own in school I had a frame of reference; I had been a Charleston County Public School student all my life. I knew how the system worked, and I knew how to pimp it. But when it came to this college stuff, my only reference was word of mouth and movies.

None of this stopped me from getting on my grind that summer after junior year. My mindset was simple, "I've got a lot of catching up to do." So that's exactly what I did! What I lacked in knowledge and resources, I compensated for with my strengths and experiences. I had an overwhelming task at hand, but I also was overly dedicated. Confidence was key that summer. Whenever I had any doubt, I would just replay in my head, "Of course Jerome's going to college."

I was nervous and unsure about my senior year, but I was ready to take new leaps of faith. An upperclassman told me, "The summer before senior year is crucial. That's the time to do all your research and line up all your applications for college." Thanks to Sara Vincelli, I knew what my mission was going to be.

I started off by focusing on schools with the best undergraduate business programs. I knew I wanted to study business, marketing specifically. My freshman year chemistry teacher, Mr. Richmond, was the first person to ever tell me that I could go to an Ivy League school. With that in the back of my mind, I had sights of doing just that, not even fully aware of all the schools that made up the Ivy League.

That's when I knew I needed to treat my college search like a research project. I discovered the University of Pennsylvania's Wharton School of Business was the best Ivy League undergraduate business program. It was in my nature to shoot for the best of the best, so UPenn quickly became my number one choice. But still, I had no clue how I was going to get there.

However, I did know I was an entrepreneur at heart. I also knew I was bold and savvy and that if I put my mind to something I get it done (just like how I wrote this book). So I used my business mindset to learn the finances of college—how much each school was going to cost, the difference between in-state, out-of-state, and private tuition, and how different schools can only meet so much of my financial need (I was broke so I needed a lot).

I then used my organization skills I learned from being a leader at school to keep track of it all—lining up scholarship deadlines for August and September, getting information packets online for each school, and adding my email to endless listservs. I also capitalized on my networking skills. If there was any card left on the table to pull, I pulled it. I talked to an old teacher over the summer who told me to send a letter to every admissions office of the schools I was looking at.

"Any document that comes to them from a student, they have to keep on file for a certain number of years… They'll have you on their radar." Looking back, I don't think this added much value, but I sent the letters anyways. He wasn't the only person I sought out advice from, either.

I spoke with another mentor that summer who told me, "Jerome, you've got to pay some of these schools a visit. At the very least, you should visit your number one choice. I think you'll regret it if you don't."

Two days after that conversation I scheduled a campus tour of the University of Pennsylvania. I had my mom drive me ten hours to Philly during the first week of August. My mentor was right. I would've regretted it. I fell in love with the school. I thought I was on my way.

By the end of that long summer, I felt like a college application pro. I knew more about *how* to apply to college than which colleges I was actually going to apply to. Collegeboard.com and Fastweb.com became my best resources. There was a point where I used those sites more than I used Google. I managed to have my early scholarship apps (the ones due in August and September) done before the school year even started. I had a list of eight schools I wanted to apply to— from my safe school to Penn. I knew I really wanted to be at a medium (five thousand to ten thousand students) sized school. I knew I wanted to go out of state. And I was sure I wanted to be at a school in some kind of an urban setting. From the outside looking in, I had it all figured out. But still I was doubtful.

Were eight schools enough? Will all this work be worth it? What if my safe schools don't even accept me? Will I get enough scholarship money? I had my heart set out on Penn. Was I aiming too high?

These questions only got louder when senior year began. Even though I had three applications done, I still had countless more to go. But I couldn't let the self-doubt take control. I also had to come to realize that I couldn't continue this massive project on my own because when school started so did DECA, Academic Bowl, AP calculus, honors English, and football. Applying to college was something I still had to take ownership over, but I also knew it was something I couldn't continue to do on my own.

It took a team to get me across the finish line. I relied heavily on English teachers, Mrs. Cannon and Mrs. Mouthaan, to review my essays. I depended on my guidance counselor, Mrs. West, to keep me up to date on all the scholarships that came out each month. I counted on Coach Stutts and Mr. Brennan for their strong letters of recommendation. And if it weren't for Mr. Beyel helping me lay out all my deadlines and keeping me honest, I don't think I would have been able to make it out of the fall semester on top. Mr. Beyel was the only person to keep me truly grounded. He assigned me soft deadlines to get my essays done in enough time for Mrs. Cannon or Mrs. Mouthaan to review them. He gave me a book with statistics and information about every school in the country. He linked my Google calendar with his so he could get alerts when due dates were approaching. And he told me to apply to Georgetown University.

"Even though I despise their basketball team," he went to Syracuse, Georgetown's biggest rival, "I think if you're looking for that Ivy League type of education with a good school-spirited atmosphere, you should apply to Georgetown." He was right. That was exactly what I was looking for, and Georgetown's business school was one of the best in the nation. I couldn't believe I overlooked them.

He told me this in October and the Georgetown application wasn't due until January, so I had time to focus on the rest of my to-do list. But during that time, my confidence was rocked. I received many rejections throughout those early months. "I regret to inform you..." and "Due to this year's competitive applicant pool..." became the most hurtful sentences of my life. I received denial letters from the QuestBridge scholarship and the Ron Brown Scholarship. I was even rejected from a small, local scholarship. But none of these denials was as hurtful as the one I got on December 15, 2014.

I came home from school that evening with my cousin, Henry. We had stopped to get food from Cookout. The classic $5 tray with a huge tea was our go-to. By the time we got to my house it was about 5:00 p.m. The sun was beginning to set. He plopped on my bed and I sat at my desk to sign in to my computer. My hands were shaking as I checked my UPenn portal. I logged in just to find yet another "no." Actually, it was a letter saying I had been waitlisted, but it might as well had been a rejection.

"You get in, bruh?"

"Nahh," I responded, a little choked up.

"Damn, I'm sorry to hear that, man."

"Yeah, me too. I'ma go get some fresh air."

With my back turned to Henry, I felt no need to resist the silent trails of disappointment that ran down my face. I was crushed. I cried to myself for about thirty minutes as I paced around my neighborhood. I had never felt like more of a failure…

In this time of self-pity, I knew I couldn't wallow in my grief for long. There was still a mission that needed to be completed. I had another application due the following week. Somehow, I found the courage to reassure myself of the immense work I had already done. I had a process going, and I needed to trust it.

In the midst of that extremely troubling time I understood what it meant to take genuine ownership over something. I knew for a fact I gave all those applications my all. I taught myself everything there was to know about college! I had no choice but to be proud of whatever work I produced because I left nothing on the table. And that's what it means to take ownership.

Taking ownership is like signing an agreement with yourself. You agree to put your best foot forward and live with whatever happens, both the good and the bad, because even if you fail, at least you'll fail controlling the controllable. By doing so, you know exactly where mistakes were made and therefore you know where to take lessons from.

My determination would eventually pay off. After $234,000 in financial aid, $70,000 in scholarships, twenty-four essays, ten months of planning, and three college trips later, I found myself with a full-ride to Georgetown University. It wasn't an easy battle, but just like the struggles I faced in third grade, I knew it was one only I could fight.

Not to be mistaken, it took a village to get me to the end, but nobody in that village worked as hard as I did, and nobody was as invested as I was. Why would they be? All those people I mentioned already had their degrees. They were only willing to put in the effort because they saw that I was too. And that's same mentality to have to adopt.

If there's something in this world that you want, you've got to have the drive to go get it. You can have all the resources in the world, but they'll all be deemed useless if you don't have the bravery to harness them, to pimp them. In everything you do, I challenge you to take accountability for it. Give everything your all and live with the outcomes. Take the initiative only you can take. Do all of these things, and you'll know what it means to take ownership.

TAKING OWNERSHIP

Darius Baxter is probably one of the most remarkable guys I've ever met who's graduated from Georgetown. At nine years old his father was shot and killed, leaving him and his brother homeless for a stretch of their life as their mother struggled to raise them on her own. What I admire most about this guy is how he was able to channel this adversity and create something GOOD...

Like most kids from similar situations, Darius knew he was going to need a "meal ticket" to remove himself from his rough environment (because so often those environments are purposefully constructed so you can't leave, thus creating a vicious cycle for most urban, minority youth). Darius found his ticket through football.

He was given the opportunity to attend Georgetown University due to his talents on the field. But his problems didn't magically disappear just because he was now at one of the top schools in the country. If anything, they only got worst. Darius will humbly admit to the deep depression he faced his freshman year of college and how he resorted to alcohol and women as his coping mechanisms of choice. It wasn't until he took ownership over his life that he was able to beat these demons.

He didn't just beat those demons, he whooped their asses! So much so, that during his senior year he decided it was going to be his life's goal to help other young people with their own internal battles. With no money, little support, and a lot of hope, Darius teamed up with two of his teammates who shared his passion for the community and created GOODProjects—a nonprofit organization dedicated to providing opportunities to underprivileged youth and their families.

"We had the ability to go out and make a difference. We just kinda answered the call," as Darius puts it. After two successful years of running a nonprofit youth organization,

I had to ask, "What are some of the most pressing issues you believe our youth are facing?" With no hesitation Darius responded, "Some of the biggest things that affect our community don't come from the outside, if I'm going to be completely honest with you. It's become very apparent in working with the communities we work with. It's going to take the community itself beginning to take pride in the rich history that we have. And we have to take ownership, not just in the physical space that we reside in, but over our own lives and our own journeys."What does that even mean? Take ownership over our lives? Are we not the sole owners of our lives already? (I thought that other stuff got abolished.) It took me a minute to fully understand this, but I eventually figured it out. You are the *only* one equipped with the necessary tools to carve your own path in this world. Leaving it up to someone else will only result in it never getting done, or worse, you leading a path that they decide for you (which is exactly the situation I found myself in chapter 5).

However, "This is the, 'I need to see it' generation," as Darius puts it, and I don't disagree. I think our generation is no longer the type to just accept whatever we hear to be fact. (If you remember anything about the election year of 2016, you'd be a fool if you did.) If you want us to believe what you're saying, you've got to put your money where your mouth is.

No more, "You need to go to college to get a good education and a good job." If I'm a young person who has never been *taught* the value of a good education but only *told* about its mystical worth, why would I place any faith at all in this statement?

Sometimes I question if college would have been as big of a priority for me if I was never exposed to the "other side." When I was fourteen years old I was named YESCarolina's Youth Entrepreneur of the Year for South Carolina after I completed the program's summer Biz-Camp. To this day, I'm still not sure I how I ended up getting this award, but I did. With this honor came a whole new world for me.

I was thrown into interviews, placed on front pages, spoke at schools, but above all I was exposed to a new world of people I never knew existed: congressmen, lawyers, mayors, business owners, millionaires, even billionaires (yeah, with a "B"). One thing most of them had in common? A college degree (they were also mostly White). That's where I learned the value of college, and it wasn't a metaphorical value either. I could put a number on it... a big one.

I'm not trying to glorify elitism or the materialistic greed that comes with the American Dream because I think that "Dream" can be just that... a dream, for too many individuals at the bottom. Because when opportunity is scarce, sometimes hard work alone is not enough (but that's a topic for a different book).

The point I am trying to make here is that it's a shame it took something so extraordinary to happen to me before I could find that ownership Darius talks about. Being the "I need to see it" generation means that if you don't come from a more affluent community, if you aren't surrounded by positive role models, if college is never a part of your peers' journey, then what you see is what you'll be. (Again, that's how I found myself in that predicament in chapter 5. Remember?) And that's not your fault. You don't get to choose your parents and you don't get to choose your environment, but you do have a say in your actions. You always have a choice in that.

Do you smoke that blunt, or do you write that paper? Do you hang out with your friends, or do you practice whatever you're passionate about? Do you pick up that extra shift, or do you give more time to studying for that test? Do you deal with your pain by yourself, or do you seek help? Do you use your situation as an excuse, or as motivation?

Now, I know these choices are easier said than done. I also don't want to be insensitive to the pressures you may be facing in your life. Smoking that blunt may be a form of self-medication to dull the pain (I began smoking weed in eighth grade); your friends may be the only people you feel close to (I thought my crew were the only ones who understood me); your family could use the money from that extra shift (I got a job at fifteen to help support my Nana); sometimes it can be hard to trust others with your feelings (I felt ashamed when talking about my mom).

But at the end of the day, those decisions, that ownership, fell on my shoulders. No one else's. At the end of the day, I knew it was my life and no one was going to care about it as much as I cared about it. So I had to find a balance. I couldn't let myself become a pothead, go to a party when I hadn't done my work, or use my screwed up childhood as a reason to be content. And neither can you.

Darius believes, "Once a young person is ready to be successful, they will be." Darius is obviously aware that it doesn't just work that easy, but what he's saying carries a lot of truth. You can't just expect success to come if you don't even want it. And wanting it, isn't enough either. Kendrick Lamar once said, "A dream is just a dream if work doesn't follow it." Just like how our communities owe it to us to put their money where their mouths are, you owe it to yourself to do the same. But like everything you do, there has to be a balance. We'll talk more about this in the last chapter.

TAKEAWAYS

Takeaway #1

My biggest piece of advice to you, when it comes to ownership, is to apply what you do know to what you don't know. Taking control of something, whether it be a facet of your life, a startup company, or your community, can always seem a bit scary, especially when it's something you've never taken the reins of before. An easy way to overcome this fear is to view it as a problem you've already solved, just under a different context. Nine times out of ten the new challenges before us are just problems we've already solved in a different way. In my case, I used my strengths from various other areas to tackle a task I hardly knew anything about.

Takeaway #2

The type of ownership I'm talking about in this chapter is very much an internal one. Most people have someone in their corner they can depend on and that's good. Support is necessary. You should cherish those people. But you should also remember that when it comes to your success, the only person who's going to put you first is you. That's why you have to take ownership over every situation you're in, even the ones you have no clue how to tackle. Always trust your abilities and all of the other assets you have to bring to the table.

Takeaway #3

Stepping up to the plate and holding yourself accountable is great, but you have to be sure you are taking ownership of things that actually matter. For example, my high school teacher, Mr. Stutts, told me the story about this one student in his class who slowly fell behind on her studies as the school year went on. Mr. Stutts knew she was an honor roll student and a bright young lady, but throughout the semester she was falling asleep more and more in his class and she even began to fail some of her assignments.

Out of concern, he addressed this issue with her one day. She told him she was getting little sleep at home because of the extra hours she was picking up at her part-time job. When he asked her if she was doing this to support her family she said, "no, not really." She was working so hard because she wanted more financial freedom from her parents, something we all can relate too. But is that "freedom" worth the expense of our grades in school?

If the livelihood of you or your family doesn't depend on it, a dead-end job shouldn't be how you choose to take ownership. Just because your job may provide you with cash now doesn't mean it will add wealth to your life later. You have the rest of your life to work. Spend this time now taking ownership over things that can pay true dividends in the future.

Attending networking events, practicing your public speaking, being a leader on campus, and maintaining a good GPA are how you should invest your time as a student. Those things will provide you with unique forms of payment later on in your life. Why spend twenty hours a week busting your ass for a couple hundred bucks if you are just going to spend it all?

Instead, you could be spending that time building a network or perfecting a craft and letting the world know you're a young person would can handle business. Take ownership over the things you care about and the things that will increase your long term human capital, not the things that are going to help you buy your twentieth pair of shoes.

CHAPTER 7

WE'RE STILL KIDS

TRUE STORY #7

Huge droplets were building at my hairline and collecting stragglers as they made their way over the ridges of my forehead. My lungs felt like stress balls, resisting to compress and decompress as I tried desperately to pump them with air. My breaths were short, and not enough. My heart was pounding louder than a bass drummer competing in his marching band's state championship—boom, boom, boom.

The throbbing vibrations made their way up to my temple. My vision blurred as I took off my glasses to rub my watery eyes. I couldn't feel it, but I saw my right hand begin to tremble like the tail end of a rattle snake. My left hand did the same, but it was fighting another battle as I struggled to not drop my new iPhone 6 that rested in my sweaty palm. I did my best to hold it firmly against my face.

By this point, it began to feel like I couldn't breathe at all now. My heart was racing even faster. My only thought was, "Oh shit, am I about to have a heart attack?" I knew I was kind of overweight, but dang, had I really eaten that many burgers? I couldn't even get the words out of my mouth to call for help. I was mute.

"Hello. Hello! Hellooo! Jerome, you can't just ignore me!" My girlfriend was on the other end of the line. She and I were in the middle of an argument before my chest decided to collapse like a bridge made of popsicle sticks. She grew impatient with my silence. Little did she know, I could barely inhale oxygen, much less utter words.

"Uhhhhhh," was all I could produce—a long, painful moan— in response to her agitation.

"Jerome, what's wrong," she was finally concerned.

I knew I had to muster up the willpower to say something, or I was going to die right there at my desk (at least that's how it felt).

"I don't know," I said followed by a short breath, "what's going on," another short breath. "My eyes are blurry," breath. "My hands are shaking," breath. "My heart is racing," breath.

"Baby, I think you're having a panic attack."

"Nmm hmm," I mumbled in disagreement.

"Yes, Jerome. Trust me. I've gotten them before. Are you sitting down?"

"Umm hmm"

"Okay, I need you to lie down on your back on the floor."

I didn't want to follow her instructions. A panic attack? I don't get panic attacks. I knew how to handle my stress. But maybe she was right, and I was willing to do anything to end this misery.

"Okay," short breath, "I'm here."

"Good. Now, close your eyes and just listen to my voice. I need you to breathe when I tell you to. Breathe in. Breathe out. Breathe in. Breathe out. Breathe in. Breathe out."

We did this back and forth for about five minutes or so. I slowly began to feel myself calm down.

"Are you okay now?"

"Yeah. Thank you. I think I need to get some rest." I was embarrassed by what just happened. And as soon as I got my wind back, I remembered the argument that caused this whole thing in the first place. I didn't want to be on the phone with her any more, so I hung up. (Yes, even after a panic attack I still found a way to be petty.)

I laid there on my dirty carpet in complete disbelief. Did that really just happen? Honestly, I wasn't that surprised. Even though I blamed her for the incident, my girlfriend was not the sole cause of this physical breakdown I just experienced. To be frank, I was shocked it hadn't happened sooner. It was the fall semester of my senior year in high school, and that was the most stressful period ever in my entire life at the time.

I was doing *everything* (or at least that's how it felt). I was the president of my school's DECA chapter. This was one of the few clubs I had been a part of since freshman year, and I was determined to leave a lasting mark. (I ended up creating an entire 5K run/walk, that still continues annually, to serve as a fundraiser for the group.) I was a school ambassador—or as the local newspaper called me "The Voice of West Ashley"— and I gave the morning announcements every day during second period.

I was captain of the academic bowl team. I was a paid motivational speaker, leaving school from time to time to inspire other students. I was the Homecoming King and male winner of the Mr. and Mrs. West Ashley Pageant. I was taking AP calculus with Mr. Brennan and honors English 4 with Mrs. Cannon. (She alone could cause any student to crumble. I love her now, though.) I was the manager of the school store—The Cat Shack. (I had to be at "work" by 6:30 a.m. every school day.) And when I wasn't managing my peers, I was working part-time at a nearby Chick-fil-A. I was also still dodging the madness of being misidentified as an opposing gang member. (Remember from chapter 5?)

I was on a variety of committees with other students and administrators, offering my leadership and insight for different task groups. I was in a long-distance relationship with a girl in college who didn't understand why I was too tired to talk on the phone every day. I guess my lack of energy had something to do with my role as a starting, varsity football player. (I hadn't figured out how to balance it yet because that was only my second year ever playing the sport.) Not to mention, my absurd aspirations of going to college. Like most seniors, I was faced with never-ending deadlines, last minute rushes to get a higher score on the SAT, and a sea of essays for scholarships and college applications. Like I said, I was doing everything.

I did all of this on top of the rest of my school work, on top of the parties, on top of trying to be "normal." And I did it all with a smile. I was the man (or, at least that's how it felt). My energy ran high, but it inevitably ran out, and I collapsed hard. Never in my wildest dreams would I think I'd be the one to catch a panic attack. I always thought those were only for the weak. For people who didn't know how to handle their circumstances.

I quickly realized that perception I held was unfair—to both those who experience these awful attacks frequently and to myself. That night taught me a very important lesson. Everyone has a breaking point. I discovered mine in one of the most terrifying ways, but now I know what that threshold is. And that's a mental limit I hope to never reach again.

I recall the days leading up to my mental health crashing. I was in Coach Stutts' classroom finishing up some last minute work for The Cat Shack. He taught the class that ran the store, and he was also the staff advisor for my DECA chapter. So, I spent a lot of time in his classroom. Me staying past the bell was a normal occurrence. I didn't mind missing half my lunch, coming in early or staying late after school for Coach.

He was my favorite teacher in high school and proved to be one of my greatest mentors. I looked up to him. Mostly because of how authentic he was. That man was weird, stern, compassionate, and blunt and he didn't care who liked or dislike him. Coach Stutts genuinely wanted me to be my best self. He always encouraged me to push myself. And even though we might have bumped heads, I always respected what he had to say.

"How long are you going to stick around here?" he asked me as I folded a shirt I had just created using our heat press machine. We had a big order to fill. This was our first year having the school's first in-house clothing company, Paw Prints, fully up and running. Paw Prints was a shirt making service now offered by The Cat Shack. We made shirts for clubs, teams, the store, fundraisers and whoever else needed an order. This was yet another of my responsibilities.

"Just gotta finish up a few more shirts. Then I'll be out of here..." I yawned, "Coach."

"Hey, man! Stop that. You're going to make me tired. It's not even one yet." I couldn't tell if he was serious or not. He always played the role of a cranky old boss, as he puts it, so I couldn't always be too sure. (No, seriously, he was an actor out in San Francisco for a few years before becoming a teacher. This was a real *role* that he enjoyed playing.)

"My bad, Coach. I guess I haven't been getting much sleep."

"C'mon, knucklehead." He shook his head in disappointment as he clicked through emails and peeled open his daily banana. "Your generation never eats right, nor do y'all get enough sleep. That's not good for your body, dude."

Another one of Coach's famous isms. I knew them all by heart.

"Yeah I know, Coach," I said as I held back the next yawn I felt coming.

"You still working nights at that chicken place?"

"Yes, sir."

"That's your problem, dude. You're doing too much. You better be careful, or else you'll burn out. And we can't afford that. You got shirts to make!"

I was staring at him the entire time. His eyes never left his computer screen, but he knew he didn't have to make eye contact with me for his message to be delivered. I heard him loud and clear. Like most of these kinds of talks with Coach Stutts, I was left pondering and annoyed because I knew he was right. Maybe I was doing too much, but there wasn't much I could do now (or at least that's how I felt). I was already overly committed, but I also knew I always had a choice—because when it comes to *your* actions, you always do.

I'm not kidding when I tell you that anxiety attack was one of the scariest things I've ever endured. Thankfully, I made it to the other side alive. Football season was over by November (we didn't make the playoffs). I changed my schedule to only work at Chick-fil-A on Saturdays. I put Mrs. Cannon's class on the back burner. (That was a risky move, though. Lowest grade I've ever gotten in high school. Almost didn't graduate—yikes!) I placed more faith in my vice president, Joey, to handle the DECA workload. When spring came, I was no longer the manager of The Cat Shack. The heated gang tension had subsided. I, unfortunately, had to end my long distance relationship. I got through all my toughest applications by the end of January, and everything else seemed to fall into place.

But, just like I told you in chapter 2, you are still the master of your own chips and how they may fall. Yes, things worked out for me, but that was because I had to remind myself who was in control. To be real, I'm still reminding myself that. I use this mindset to make sure I'm balancing my life. I deserve prosperity, and I owe it to myself to work hard for what I want, but I also ought to relish in my youth and have fun. I'm entitled to my desires, but I also should not get caught up in the falsehood that I need some incredible résumé before I can even legally drink just to be successful.

Having high expectations and big dreams are never a bad thing. In fact, I encourage them. Your goals should be so big that you feel uncomfortable telling smallminded people. Your dreams should be so gigantic that they scare you! I know mine do. One of my biggest dreams since I was sixteen years old was to write this book, and as I write it, I'm terrified. I'm afraid that you won't like what I have to say. Or that my words won't inspire you or touch you in some way, but I'm writing it anyway because somehow I've found the courage to follow my heart. And I know that this book has the potential to change at least one life.

This is exactly how you should feel about all your major aspirations and goals. That's a healthy feeling. I'm not saying don't let your ambitions push you; I'm saying don't let them push you too far. Just like how negativity can crush your spirits, being spread too thin can crush your mental health. Some students try to do everything, and some students don't have the drive to do anything. I'm telling you that the best place to be is in the middle.

A friend once told me, "I can't complain about what's on my plate if my goal is to eat." I thought that was a great quote, and I still do to a certain degree. But this is how I interpret it. She's right. If you have a true drive and a passion and a hunger for success, then yes, you shouldn't complain about what type of food is on your metaphorical plate. You don't control what the buffet has to offer, just like how you don't control what life has to offer.

However, you can control how much of that food, whatever it may be, to place on your plate, just like how you control your actions in this world. And sometimes our eyes are bigger than our stomachs. Remember, you're only human. You require sleep, food, good energy, exercise, and happiness like the rest of us. Coach Stutts helped me realize that no one expects young people to have it all figured out, and if someone is putting that kind of pressure on you, they're a jackass. I mean that too.

There is a difference between accepting ignorance and accepting that you just don't know everything. One is being a fool, and the other is a path toward wisdom. By choosing the latter, you are committing yourself to always working hard and searching for truth while being self-aware of your limitations and how little you actually know.

From what I've shared, you can see that I clearly wasn't aware of my limits (or didn't want to face them), but I was open minded enough to listen to those I trusted when they told me where I was falling blind. From this experience I learned to run my own race, and you have to uncover what you race looks like.

And in all honesty, most of these "adults" around here don't have it all figured out either, so why should you?

WE'RE STILL KIDS

When I asked Allison Hilton what some of the biggest challenges she believes young people are facing today are, she immediately said, "I feel like so often, especially in our marginalized communities, our young people aren't given the time to be young people."

Allison has been working to improve the lives of youth for the past seven years, and when she said that, I really wanted to know exactly what she meant. Recently, she moved back home to Charleston to assist the youth of the Lowcountry, but before that, Allison spent over five years working for Georgetown University's After School Kids (ASK) Program, which is dedicated to tutoring court-involved youth and helping them prepare for successful lives as adults. (Allison actually recruited me to be a tutor for ASK the summer *before* I even got to Georgetown. Crazy right? I guess it's a Charleston thing though. You wouldn't understand.)

Allison shared with me a touching story of a young man she met who had just joined the ASK Program when he was about sixteen or seventeen years old. As Allison puts it, "When he started, he didn't care about literally *anything.*" You can only imagine how difficult it must've been to work and try to help a student so disinterested. He was in the program because he got caught boosting cars, and it got to the point that the only way Allison could engage with the young man was by putting things in "street" metaphors. She met him half way.

The student told Allison one day, "Ya'll just tryna finesse me into doing my work."

"You feel like it's finessing you to do your work, but if you go steal somebody's van and you want a $1,000 for it, and somebody says 'Nah, I'm only going to give you $300,' do you feel like they're finessing you? Or do you feel like you're finessing them by wanting $1,000?"

"No, I just want my $1,000."

"Okay, well then we're just here to do our jobs. If your job is boosting cars, and that's what you have to do, then our job is to get you tutored, and that's what we have to do."

And that's why Allison is so good at what she does. Once she put things into his context, she was able to connect with the young man and move forward. After two years, they were able to move from him being completely disengaged to him asking, "What can I do to better myself?" He was now eighteen and his time with the program was coming to an end.

"Well, what do you wanna do? What do you like to do?" is what Allison asked him during his final days in the ASK Program.

Confused, the student responded with, "What do you mean, 'what do I like to do'?"

"Like, what are your hobbies?"

He looked back at Allison, even more confused than before, and asked "What do you mean 'hobbies'? I don't do anything for fun."

That's when Allison discovered that his entire life had been focused on stealing to survive. He had to rob others to provide for not only himself, but for his family too. Most of the time his role within his family was flipped, and he spent much of his childhood providing for his mother instead of the other way around. What's most heartbreaking about his story is that he never had time to be a kid.

He didn't have the time to hang outside and play basketball. Hey didn't have the opportunity to try different things; to find out what he liked or what he disliked. He had one objective growing up. It was always about survival. He was just, "out in the world existing." Now, at the age of eighteen, he had very little direction to guide him. Allison says that's when she realized, "These young people don't really have anywhere to go."

If this young man reminds you of yourself, you have to remember—you're still a kid. I don't mean that in a demeaning way either. I know fifteen-year-olds who are forced to get a job and provide for their families (that was me). When I was fourteen, I became the man of the house. I was forced to discipline my younger brother, cook dinner when my Nana was at her second job, and even pay a bill or two.

So trust me, I know these are not the responsibilities of a "kid," but you still deserve to enjoy your youth. (That's what

I've been preaching this whole chapter.) Granted, you may not be stealing to survive and your circumstances may not be nearly as severe as this young man's, but we all can relate to finding ourselves in a rush to grow up. As a "kid" who's aging out of his youth, I can tell you, you have your whole life to be an adult. But soon, your innocence, inquisitiveness, and energy will run short. Unless your livelihood depends on it, you should not be in any rush to waste these intuitions on anything but the things you love and enjoy doing. And let's be honest, no one *really* enjoys working at a burger joint in high school.

On the other hand, if this young man is nothing like you, be sure to not to waste the freedom you have to just be a kid. We live in a very unfair world where some have everything, and some have nothing. However, not having, or being blissfully unaware of, the pressures that can come with domestic violence, low-income communities, racist institutions, or broken homes is one of the greatest privileges any young person can have.

If these forces aren't affecting your life directly, there's no reason why you shouldn't be basking in your youth. Spend this time mastering a craft or pursuing a passion. (Trust me, this is the most time you'll ever have until you retire!) I know for me, I wish I spent more time reading books and learning more about film while I was in high school. Looking back on it all, I had a ton of free time before I got to college, even amidst all the messed-up stuff I had to go through.

All I'm saying is don't let the world rob you of your youth. We're still kids.

RESPECTING OUR ELDERS

Has anyone ever told you that you need to practice more filial piety? If I had to guess, probably not. But I'm sure at some point in your life you've been told to respect your elders. Well, that's exactly what filial piety means. Many cultures teach their young to appreciate and listen to their elders. What you may not know is that this an ideology that goes way beyond just Western culture. Confucius, an ancient Chinese philosopher, was the first to coin filial piety, which is the virtue of respect for one's parents, elders, and ancestors.

Although, it doesn't matter if you're in America, China, or Turkey, young people across the world struggle with this ancient virtue. But as young people, we owe it to ourselves to respect and listen to the older, wiser generations above us. Millennials are projected to be the most educated generation in history. But a college degree does not mean we're wise. In some cases, it doesn't even mean we're smart either. There's still a lot that can be learned outside of a classroom. In fact most of life's biggest lessons are not taught in school.

Dr. Sylvia Önder has been teaching Turkish Language and Culture at Georgetown since the Fall of 1998. She also teaches an Anthropology and Youth Culture course. When I asked her about the relationship between youth and their elders, she told me a very interesting story of her time in Turkey.

She conducted her anthropological study in a rural area of Turkey, on a farm. What she found was that "everyone was trying to get their kid off to college." I was intrigued to hear this. Who would've known that college was just as big of a concern in Turkey as it is in the US. However, this glamorization of higher education has created a rift within Turkish culture.

"The problem with farming is that nobody respects what farmers know. Everybody thinks a machine could do it." What Professor Önder said next was even more surprising. "And so, because farmers' knowledge is not respected, no farmers want their kids to be a farmer."

As a result, you can find these rural children multitasking between studying their vocabulary words and taking care of the cow while the old folks are doing the manual labor. This disconnect is creating a void among the Turks.

Professor Önder gave me an example of a farmer she met who knows how to graft different branches of fruit trees together. Grafting is basically a surgical process of inserting the branch of one particular tree into the trunk of another so they can grow as one. When she explained this concept to me I was amazed.

"So, let's take a pear tree," she said. "A pear tree has a season. It blooms and then the pears form where the flowers grow. But what if you want more pears than that? You can take a different pear's branch and graft it onto your pear tree, and then you can have two different kinds of pears growing in different seasons."

My mind was blown! She told me this guy was so good at his craft that he had up to ten different kinds of pears on one tree.

"Wow, I didn't know that was even a thing!"

"Well, nobody does. Because it's just farmers that do stuff like that." She continued by saying, "So, when he dies, people aren't going to even know that you can do that kind of thing.

Because none of his kids learned it. They were all in school trying to become businessmen or whatever."

In my short conversation with Professor Önder, I learned an incredible lesson. We as adolescents in America are no different than those in Turkey. Much like the Turkish kids, we too do not always value the wisdom our elderly have to offer, particularly those without a college education. Even the high school seniors I mentor at Duke Ellington School of the Arts in Washington, DC, have told me they think their current generation is too entitled.

"Yeah they empower us too much," one of my mentees said as he chuckled in his chair. "Always telling us that 'The world is in our hands.'" He let out a hard laugh. "I don't know shit!"

I don't completely agree with Destine. Young people have gone on to do some amazing things in this world, but there is some truth to what he's saying. Why do we feel like we know everything? Professor Önder says it has a lot to do with "when the whole culture decides that kids shouldn't do what their parents did."

In the past, most kids followed their parents' profession. In fact, that's how some families got their surnames—because of their occupation. The Wallers were masons, the Smiths were metal workers, and the Chandlers were candle makers (fun fact, right?). However, if we say that family occupations are bad and that "nobody should follow in their parents' footsteps," we might as well be saying "everyone's family is worthless."

To be clear, I understand that every parent wants their child to be better off in life than they were. We live in the twenty-first century. You aren't confined to being a fisherman just because your last name is Fisher. But if we continue to think that those with college educations are the only ones with the answers, we are bound to be a generation of fools. Our elders have lessons to share that could change our lives. We shouldn't be knuckleheads and continue to deny this. Between you and me, I've gotten some of the best advice from hardworking folk who didn't even have a high school diploma.

Our parents and grandparents may not have been farmers, but they have lived full lives. We need to recognize that we're still kids, and there is much we can learn from them. I say "we" because this is something I struggle with myself. Nevertheless, I've come to acknowledge the value that our elders can provide. And even though I've been speaking mostly about family, those I consider to be our elders is not limited to who we're related to. Elders can come in the form of a teacher, a family friend, a neighbor, and especially a mentor.

If it weren't for the mentors in my life I don't know where I'd be. When I was younger I was mature enough to know that these people had interesting stories about life and about how they overcame tough obstacles. I knew if I listened, truly listened, there was always going to be a nugget of wisdom I could apply to my life. And I'm sure the adults in your life have plenty of nuggets of wisdom that you can use too.

SAVE THE WORLD, AND YOURSELF

Youth across the globe believe they can change the world. Given the current political climate, I don't disagree. I think often times our energy complements our activism. It's especially beautiful to see adults, who are well into their careers, still living by the same passions they had when they were younger. Dr. John Wright is one of those adults.

Dr. Wright is a licensed psychologist and Assistant Director for Diversity Initiatives at Georgetown University's Counseling and Psychiatric Services.

Much like us, he was also an ambitious youth back when he was in college, but that wasn't always the case. Dr. Wright has one of the most incredible stories I've ever heard. As he puts it, he grew up in a family situation that would have gobbled most people up and spit them out. In my eyes, he is the definition of a flower that grew from concrete. When he was just four years old, his mother was deemed unfit to raise him and the state claimed custody. From that point on, his life would prove to be an uphill battle.

Dr. Wright spent the rest of his juvenile years in foster care—four different homes to be exact. For the next thirteen years, until he turned seventeen, Dr. Wright told me all he could think about during that time was, "survival."

"In hindsight, during those points in my life, there were people that had some kind of significant impact on me that literary saved me…"

One of those people was his high school guidance counselor, who changed his life. He was walking through the halls of Eastside High when one day she pulled him into her office. She sat him down across from her desk and told him, "I've been watching you for a couple years." Then, she looked him in the eyes and said, "I know you're better than that."

He had never interacted with this woman before that day. He had no idea why she was doing this, but he believed what she said. And for the first time, he believed in himself. This mini pep-talk wasn't why she pulled him to the side, but what followed would change his life forever.

She laid out three recently opened letters on top of her mahogany desk. He looked down at the letters, and then back at her with a slightly puzzled face, still, with no clue of exactly what was going on. Each envelope had the seal of a different college logo. She went on to tell him that for the past few months, she had been submitting college applications on his behalf. Because of his living situations, she was able to get the letters sent to the school. What she just placed before him were three schools he had been accepted to. Three different chances at a better life.

He looked at her in disbelief. He was shocked. The hard thumping of her index finger on the desk was what brought him back to reality. She was tapping on one of the letters in particular. "That one. You're going to go here," she told him.

"She sent me to Rutgers!" It was almost as if, even thirty years later, he still couldn't believe it.

Dr. Wright had no intention of going to college, and if it wasn't for his guidance counselor, he wouldn't have. She sent him to Rutgers University because of its Equal Opportunity Funding Program. All he had to do was stay in good academic standing and his four years would be completely paid for.

The problem with this program was that it didn't offer any real support beyond a financial one. Out of the 160 students who started off with Dr. Wright in the EOF Program, more than half of them dropped out within the first two years. The reason? There was no academic, emotional, or physical support offered.

It broke his heart to see so many of his peers not make it to the end, so he found ways to help the ones who were still there. He joined clubs and created initiatives that built community among students of color on campus. This urge to give back came naturally, he says. Over time, this urge began to feel more and more like an obligation.

Thinking back on his life, a young Dr. Wright, felt a sense of "unearned privilege" during his time at Rutgers. "Why me?" he would ask himself. In many ways, he felt ordinary. He felt like he didn't deserve to be there. He believed that it could have been anyone who got this lucky break. As result, an odd feeling of survivor's remorse began to weigh on his heart.

This pushed him into the career path of psychology. His mission was simple—provide the mental and emotional support, that he was not afforded, to students of color in higher education.

Dr. Wright told me, "I literary feel like the sequences in my life have led me to this." And that's why he doesn't consider his role as a job. He says, "It's a calling."

———

This "calling" has continued to push Dr. Wright for the past three decades. In addition to his role as a therapist on Georgetown's campus, Dr. Wright also teaches classes at the University of the District of Columbia and leads a variety of community outreach programs throughout DC. In short, he's a busy man.

Over the years, though, Dr. Wright has discovered firsthand how too much of a good thing may not be such a good thing. After hearing a story like his, it's no wonder why Dr. Wright is so incredibly motivated to give back and pay it forward. His appreciation for those who gave him a fighting chance is why he's passionate about providing the same level of investment within the lives of others. However, he warned me that being driven and compelled toward a greater purpose can be a very dangerous thing.

"It may be my passion that actually kills me," he said, "but I can't imagine a life where I'm not giving."

That line spoke to me a lot because I resonated with it so much. At first I internalized it as being willing to die for what you believe in. But being ready to die for what you believe in and allowing what you believe in to kill you are two different things.

Dr. Wright didn't take his first vacation until he was forty years old. Even his doctor told him he needs to be more mindful of his health, but he says he can't stop. This has been how he serves his community since he was in college. He's reached the point of no return; he doesn't know how to function any other way.

But just because it's too late for him doesn't mean it's too late for you. Dr. Wright told me he wishes he had someone in his life giving him advice on how to balance his mental health with a life of service. That's why he's honest with every student he encounters, encouraging them not to follow his methods and to find healthier ways to being agents of social change.

As students, we can feel empowered to go out and change the world. But our youthful energy can provide a false sense of invincibility. We all have a limit. And we have to learn ways to put ourselves first, even before our most meaningful passions. It's okay to want to save the world, but you have to be sure you're saving yourself in the process.

TAKEAWAYS

Takeaway #1

First things first, find ways to embrace your youth! I told you my story of being spread too thin, and Allison's story of working with a young man who was literally living to survive. Unlike Allison's mentee, I had a choice in how I chose to spend my time, and my decisions led me to a mental breakdown. With that said, if you have the option to just be a kid, do it.

Takeaway #2

A part of embracing your youth is finding ways to still have fun and do the things that you love while also using your youthfulness as a resource. Being young becomes our greatest asset when seeking mentorship. This falls under respecting our elders. Understanding that our short-lived experiences can be enhanced by the wisdom of those older than us is the first step. The second step is understanding that older adults are dying to share knowledge with us.

Most people want to give back to the community in some way, but either don't have the time or don't know how. That's why they get so excited when a young person asks them for advice. They view this as their way of giving back. Allow people to support you and be open to new ideas from the ones we've been told to respect our whole lives.

Takeaway #3

The biggest takeaway I want you to get from this chapter is to avoid burnout by not spreading yourself too thin. Yes, we are young and full of life, but stamina is not synonymous with indestructible. Everything and everyone has a limit, including you. We cannot get caught up in the notion of "I'll sleep when I'm dead." Everything in this world is about balance, and you just have to find yours.

For someone like Dr. Wright, he's too invested. Yet, that's the way he's decided to contribute to the world. It's an honorable choice, but it's also dangerous. If you think back to my situation senior year, I had so much on my plate to the point that it affected my physical health. I made a promise to never reach that limit again. That's why I make it a priority to practice self-care and to find outlets where I can talk about what's going on in my life.

I've also grown enough to know when and where to cut back on my obligations (some things just need to take the back burner). Much like the remedy I use for when I'm feeling lost, I use this process to cope with the pressures and obligations of life. If you don't have one yet, you should spend some time thinking about what you want your own process to look like. Even though you may not need it now, there is going to come a time when you'll feel close to the edge of burnout. The easiest way to avoid that is to have a healthy process that you call your own.

ACKNOWLEDGMENTS

I must start off by taking the time to thank you—my reader. You were, by no means, obligated to read *Small Talk*, yet you did anyway and that deserves recognition. I didn't write this book for the money (I'm giving the proceeds away); nor did I write this book for myself (this is not an autobiography). I wrote this book for you. And if my words hold the power to impact at least one life, my mission will be fulfilled.

I want to give an enormous thank you to Allison Hilton, Amit Dodani, Cordelia Cranshaw, Darius Baxter, Devita Bishundat, Emily Kaye, Haley Bauer, Jim Cantoni, Kenneth Joyner, Marc Steren, Missy Foy, Sylvia Önder, Tamica Coleman, Tanmay Rao, and all my little homies at Duke Ellington School of the Arts for allowing me to interview you and gain perspective on the issues that face our youth today.

I dedicated *Small Talk* to every young person without a mentor because I know if it weren't for the men and women I had guiding me along the way, I wouldn't be half the man I am today. With that said, thank you to all of my mentors who have supported me throughout my journey. A special thank you to my grandfather, Jimmy Bailey, and Terry Stutts, for not only assisting me through life but for also giving me a helping hand with this project.

I'd like to also thank my high school English teacher, Sandra Cannon, for taking the time to be an advanced reader of *Small Talk* and providing me with the honest feedback I needed to make this thing special.

I would be remiss not to give thanks to my wise and thoughtful brother, Dr. John Wright. You were the driving force that got me to the finish line when I was at my lowest. Your words of encouragement pushed me during that difficult time when I was deeply lost in the sauce. Because of you, I began to accept *Small Talk* as a living, breathing body of work that I needed to learn how to "live with," and thank God I did.

Thank you to the craziest, most empowering professor I've ever had, Eric Koester. If it wasn't for your class, I don't believe *Small Talk* would have ever come about. You brought my dream to reality and continued to fight for me every step of the way, even though I was never on time for a single deadline for the publisher. Words cannot describe how much I appreciated all of your insane ideas and immense insight.

I want to thank all of my friends who have supported me throughout this journey. There were times when y'all saw something in me that I did not see in myself. I want you all to know that your messages of love and affirmation did not go unnoticed. Each text, snap, call, or FaceTime meant the world to me, and I wanted you to know that.

Last, but certainly not least, thank you to Mama and my Nana, the two strongest women I've ever had in my life, for finding the courage to love me unconditionally and to raise a man with your tender love and care. I love you both with all my heart.

REFERENCES

Lamar, Kendrick, writer. *To Pimp a Butterfly*. Top Dawg Entertainment / Aftermath Records / Interscope Records, 2015, CD.

Brown, Brene. "The Power of Vulnerability." Speech. June 2010.